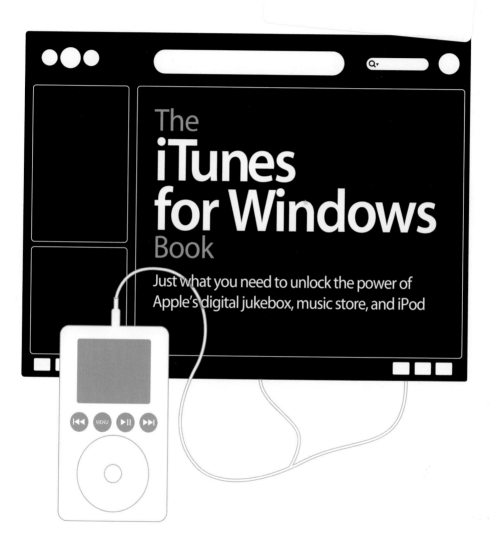

The
iTunes
for Windows
Book

Just what you need to unlock the power of
Apple's digital jukebox, music store, and iPod

Scott Kelby • Kleber Stephenson

The team behind the best-selling book Windows XP Killer Tips

The iTunes for Windows Book

The iTunes for Windows Book Team

TECHNICAL EDITORS
Jorge Sanchez
Chris Main

COPY EDITOR
Daphne Durkee

PRODUCTION EDITOR
Kim Gabriel

PRODUCTION
Dave Damstra
Dave Korman

COVER DESIGN AND
CREATIVE CONCEPTS
Felix Nelson

SITE DESIGN
Stacy Behan

PUBLISHED BY
Peachpit Press

Copyright © 2004 by Scott Kelby

FIRST EDITION: February 2004

Composed in Myriad, Lucida Grande, and Helvetica by NAPP Publishing

Trademarks
All terms mentioned in this book that are known to be trademarks or service marks have been appropriately capitalized. Peachpit Press cannot attest to the accuracy of this information. Use of a term in the book should not be regarded as affecting the validity of any trademark or service mark.

iPod, iTunes, Mac, and Macintosh are trademarks of Apple Computer, Inc., registered in the United States and other countries.

Windows is a registered trademark of Microsoft Corporation.

Warning and Disclaimer
This book is designed to provide information about iTunes for Windows. Every effort has been made to make this book as complete and as accurate as possible, but no warranty of fitness is implied.

The information is provided on an as-is basis. The authors and Peachpit Press shall have neither liability nor responsibility to any person or entity with respect to any loss or damages arising from the information contained in this book or from the use of the discs or programs that may accompany it.

ISBN 0-321-26744-3

9 8 7 6 5 4 3 2

Printed and bound in the United States of America

www.peachpit.com
www.scottkelbybooks.com

For Felix Nelson:
One of the most talented, creative, fun,
and genuine individuals I've ever known.
–SCOTT KELBY

For my best friend and wife, Debbie;
every day with you reminds me how fortunate
I was to be lucky enough to marry you.
–KLEBER STEPHENSON

Acknowledgments

Scott Kelby

Although only two names appear on this book's spine, it takes a large, dedicated team of people to put a book like this together. Not only did I have the good fortune of working with such a great group of people; I now get the great pleasure of thanking them and acknowledging their hard work and tireless dedication.

First I'd like to thank my wonderful, amazing, hilarious, fun-filled, and loving wife, Kalebra. You're the best thing that's ever happened to me—you're part wonderwoman, part supermom, part business exec, and part stand-up comic, and every day you manage to put a smile on my lips and a song in my heart. Your spirit, warmth, beauty, patience, and unconditional love continue to prove what everybody always says—I'm the luckiest guy in the world.

I also want to thank my son, Jordan. I'm so proud of him, so thrilled to be his dad, and I love watching him turn into the wonderful "little man" he has become. He has so many of his mother's special gifts, especially her boundless heart, and it's amazing the amount of joy he and his mom bring into my life. I'm very grateful God has blessed me with them.

Special thanks go to Kleber, my co-author and good friend, whose invaluable contributions to the book helped make it better than it ever would have been. If only our Buccaneers had at least made the playoffs this year, well…this really could have been a banner year for us.

To Felix Nelson, for his seemingly nonstop flow of creative ideas and input, which make every book we do that much better. (He's also the most solid bass player the modern world has ever known, but like all things, he's pretty modest about that, too.)

To Dave Moser for never letting a good idea lie dormant for more than 20 seconds, and for his goal of making sure that everything we do is better than anything we've done.

Thanks and much love to my amazing crew at KW Media Group, especially my "Main" man Chris Main, Barbara Thompson, Daphne Durkee, Dave Damstra, Sarah Hughes, Kim Gabriel, Stacy Behan, Dave Korman, Ronni O'Neil, and Margie from New York. You guys are the best (I'm not just saying that, and it's not just me that thinks it).

I want to give a special thanks to all my friends at Peachpit Press, especially my editor, Steve Weiss, and my publisher, Nancy Ruenzel. They really "get it" and their philosophy and vision make writing books an awful lot of fun, which is very rare in this industry. Also thanks to Scott Cowlin, Gary Paul Price, Stephanie Wall, and a special thanks to Rachel Tiley at New Riders (the real power behind the throne).

I couldn't do any of this without the help and support of my wonderful assistant, Kathy Siler, who is so happy that Coach Joe Gibbs is back to coach her Redskins that anything else I say is pretty much irrelevant.

Thanks to to my brother, Jeff, for being such an important part of my life, and for his many great ideas and contributions throughout my life. To my wonderful, happy, crazy father, Jerry, the dad all other dads should be judged by, whose true love of life and love of people continues to be an inspiration to us all.

Thanks to the whole team at KW Media Group, for their committment to excellence, for refusing to accept limitations, and for being an example of what's best about this industry.

To my friends and business partners, Jim Workman and Jean A. Kendra, for their support and enthusiasm for all my writing projects.

And most importantly, an extra special thanks to God and His son Jesus Christ for always hearing my prayers, for always being there when I need Him, and for blessing me with a wonderful life I truly love and such a warm, loving family to share it with.

Kleber Stephenson

Debbie Stephenson:
You're not only the most beautiful woman I've ever seen, but you're an amazing mother and my best friend. Thanks for always being patient and understanding, and for your endless encouragement. You're the most special thing about me.

Jarod Stephenson:
"My Little Guy": You're the absolute coolest person I know. It still amazes me how a five-year-old can be so tough, thoughtful, funny, and wise. I hope to be just like you when I grow up.

Jenna Stephenson:
"My Little Princess": I love looking at the world through your eyes. You see wonder in things that most people could never see. You make everything more beautiful, and I just couldn't make it through a day without your "snuggles."

Kleber and Barbara Stephenson:
Mom and Dad, I can never thank the two of you enough. Your remarkable care and selflessness comes so naturally that you don't even realize how extraordinary and amazing it is. You're both a blessing to everyone you've ever met.

My Sisters:
Most guys would think growing up with four sisters (Cheryl Lucas, Kalebra Kelby, Julie Stephenson, and Heidi Crist) would have been miserable. Well it was, and I hold every single one of you responsible for every neurotic episode that I might ever have—just kidding (kind of). I love all of you very much and will eventually be able to say that out loud and with a straight face. ;-) All kidding aside, you're all amazing women and I'm extremely fortunate to have the four of you for sisters.

Scott Kelby:
It's never work working with you. It's more like hanging out in a comedy club with a 12-drink minimum. You have a very rare drive and enthusiasm for everything you do that makes people enjoy just being around you, and I'm definitely one of those people.

Dave Moser:
Well, Commissioner, the "Bat Phone" is active. Thanks for everything, especially for your help and support, and great ideas!

KW Media Group:
A special thanks to Felix Nelson, Dave Damstra and Kim Gabriel. All of you are extremely talented people who make producing books appear ridiculously easy. Thanks for your professionalism and very hard work.

The Lord, Jesus Christ:
Lastly, but most importantly I want to thank God. God has blessed me more than I deserve and I feel him in my life every day. Thank you for your forgiveness (you know I need it), understanding, blessings, and guidance.

About The Authors

Scott Kelby

Scott is Editor-in-Chief and co-founder of *Photoshop User* magazine, Editor-in-Chief of Nikon's *Capture User* magazine, and Editor-in-Chief of *Mac Design Magazine*. He is President of the National Association of Photoshop Professionals (NAPP), the trade association for Adobe® Photoshop® users, and President of KW Media Group, Inc., a Florida-based software education and publishing firm.

Scott is author of the best-selling books *Photoshop CS Down & Dirty Tricks* and *The Photoshop CS Book for Digital Photographers,* and he's creator and series Editor for the Killer Tips series from New Riders Publishing. Scott has authored several best-selling Macintosh books, including *Mac OS X Panther Killer Tips* and the award-winning *Macintosh: The Naked Truth,* both also from New Riders, and *Mac OS X Conversion Kit: 9 to 10 Side by Side* from Peachpit Press.

Scott introduced his first software title in 2003 called "Kelby's Notes for Adobe Photoshop," which provides the answers to the 100 most-asked Photoshop questions, accessed from directly within Photoshop.

Scott is Training Director for the Adobe Photoshop Seminar Tour, Conference Technical Chair for the PhotoshopWorld Conference & Expo, and a speaker at graphics trade shows and events around the world. He is also featured in a series of Adobe Photoshop training videos and DVDs and has been training Adobe Photoshop users since 1993.

For more background on Scott, visit www.scottkelby.com.

Kleber Stephenson

Kleber is President of U.S. Diginet–Interactive Communications, an award-winning, full-service provider of Internet solutions, integrated strategy consulting, and secure, stable hosting environments for growing e-business enterprises.

Kleber is also President of Medical Assisted Services, Inc., a Florida-based medical company with several divisions, providing diagnostic testing services, pain-management solutions, and durable medical equipment to physicians and health care professionals throughout the U.S.

He is also a contributing technology reviewer for *Mac Design Magazine* and *Photoshop User*, and has more than a decade of experience analyzing and implementing business computing infrastructures based on the Windows platform. Through his existing businesses, Kleber designs and develops real-world network and administrative solutions based on Microsoft technologies and the Windows OS architecture.

Kleber lives in the Tampa Bay area of Florida with his wife, Debbie, his son, Jarod, and his daughter, Jenna.

Table of Contents

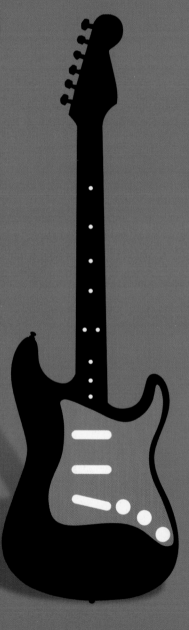

Chapter One 1

Get the Party Started

ITUNES ESSENTIALS

Playing a Song   2
Who's Singing the Song?   3
Adding Your Own Song Info   4
Finding Your Playlist's Total Running Time   5
Groovin' with Meters   6
Controlling Information Overload   7
Faster Column Views   8
Changing a Song's Name. Or Artist. Or...   9
Delete a Song from iTunes   10
Delete Multiple Songs from iTunes   11
Rearranging the Song Order   12
User-Friendly Columns   13
A-to-Z or Z-to-A   14
Finding the Currently Playing Song   15
A Better iTunes Window   16
It's Mini-Tunes   17

Chapter Two 19

We Can Work It Out

WORKING WITH SONGS

Pump Up the Volume   20
Stop the Highs and Lows   21
iTunes' Built-In EQ   22
Saving Your Own Custom EQs   23
A Different EQ for Every Song   24
Apply EQ Settings to Groups of Songs   25
You Can Control iTunes from Here   26
Add Album Artwork to Your Songs   27
Play It Again and Again and...   28
The All On, All Off Shortcut   29
Crossfade Between Songs   30
Adding Songs to Your iTunes Library   31

Chapter Three   33
Quit Playing Games with My Heart
PLAYING WITH PLAYLISTS

Create a Playlist	34
Delete Songs from a Playlist	35
Delete a Playlist	36
How to Skip over a Song in Your Playlist	37
Smart Playlists Really Are Smart	38
My Top 10, Automatically	39
Shortcut for Creating Smart Playlists	40
Create a Playlist from a Selection	41
Everybody's a Critic: Rating Songs	42
A Five-Star Playlist	43
A Window of Its Own	44
Reset a Song's Play Count	45
Combine Playlists	46
Exporting Your Playlists	47

Chapter Four   49
Sort It Out
ORGANIZING YOUR MUSIC

Can't Find Your Songs?	50
Browsing Is a Breeze	51
Browsing by Genre	52
Bring Order to iTunes	53
Come Together	54
Add Custom and Multiple Genres	55
Font Super-Sizing	56
Get to the Good Stuff: Editing Out Long, Boring Intros	57
Editing a Bunch of Songs at Once	58
Quick Ratings	59
Locate Your Songs	60

Table of Contents

Chapter Five   **63**

Can't Buy a Thrill

THE ITUNES MUSIC STORE

My iTunes Music Store Wish List	64
iTunes on a Budget	65
Tell a Friend	66
Better Song Previews for Dial-Up Users	67
"Deauthorize" Your Computer	68
Linking to Songs in the Store from Your Webpage	69
Spoiling Your Kids...Automatically	70
Music Preview Shortcut	71
The Shortcut to Finding More of an Artist's Work	72
The ITMS's Hidden Links	73
What to Do If the "Buy Now" Button Says "Add Song"	74
The Home Page Navigation Dots	75
Ready for a "Power Search"?	76
Find an Artist's Website	77
Don't Use the Back Button. Shortcut It.	78
Don't Just Search: Browse	79
Sort Your Searches	80
Keep Other People from Buying on Your Computer	81
How Much Have You Bought?	82
Can't Remember Which Songs Were Hot That Year?	83
If You're Sharing Music, They Won't Hear ITMS-Downloaded Songs	84
Getting Faster ITMS Song Previews	85

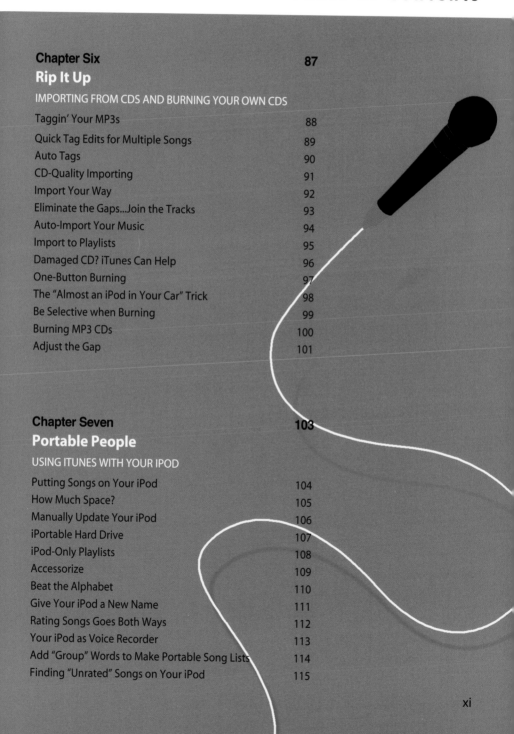

Chapter Six   87
Rip It Up
IMPORTING FROM CDS AND BURNING YOUR OWN CDS

Taggin' Your MP3s	88
Quick Tag Edits for Multiple Songs	89
Auto Tags	90
CD-Quality Importing	91
Import Your Way	92
Eliminate the Gaps...Join the Tracks	93
Auto-Import Your Music	94
Import to Playlists	95
Damaged CD? iTunes Can Help	96
One-Button Burning	97
The "Almost an iPod in Your Car" Trick	98
Be Selective when Burning	99
Burning MP3 CDs	100
Adjust the Gap	101

Chapter Seven   103
Portable People
USING ITUNES WITH YOUR IPOD

Putting Songs on Your iPod	104
How Much Space?	105
Manually Update Your iPod	106
iPortable Hard Drive	107
iPod-Only Playlists	108
Accessorize	109
Beat the Alphabet	110
Give Your iPod a New Name	111
Rating Songs Goes Both Ways	112
Your iPod as Voice Recorder	113
Add "Group" Words to Make Portable Song Lists	114
Finding "Unrated" Songs on Your iPod	115

Table of Contents

Chapter Eight   **117**

Silver Screen Shower Scene

ITUNES VISUALS

Get Funky   118

Maximize Your Funk   119

iLogo (The Hidden Corporate Message)   120

Visual Effects   121

Who's Playing?   122

One-Key Control   123

Gettin' Geeky with Visuals   124

Plug In to Visual Effects   125

Chapter Nine   **127**

Advanced Deviation

ADVANCED ITUNES

Tuning In to iTunes   128

Hey, Who Did That Song?   129

My Favorite Radio Stations   130

It's Good to Share   131

Keep It Simple—Import Your Playlists   132

Another Way to Shuffle   133

Convert Your Songs   134

Skipping this brings bad karma
(and perhaps jail time)

You're pulling my leg, right?
Absolutely (about the jail time part. Not the karma part). Because if you skip this all-important, albeit brief introduction, you could experience a phenomenon known as "Instant Karma" (and believe us, you don't want instant—hold out for the brewed kind).

Look, if you really want us to be straight with you, we'll be straight with you—nobody reads book introductions anymore. Nobody. Anything called the "Introduction" is read so little that even the book's editors and proofreaders won't read it. That's why writers have come up with ways to trick readers into reading their introductions. They name them "Chapter 0" or "Read This First" or "Ancient Euro-Asian Sex Manual" or one of a dozen or so common ruses just to get you to read their introductions. So why do authors go through all this trouble? There are two reasons: (1) Publishers force authors to write these introductions (knowing full well that no one will read it, or even proofread it) and (2) it helps the overall page count. It's mostly #2.

OK, there's probably a third reason—it gives the author a chance to tell the reader what makes this book different, how to use the book, how to get the most out of the book, how to send a tax-deductible contribution to the author, where to send the author bail money, and a host of other little tidbits designed to make the whole thing a better experience for you.

In fact, once you write a book yourself, you then realize how important these oft-overlooked introductions are, so you start reading them in every book you buy (if you can get past all the typos due to no real editing or proofreading whatsoever). So, if you've come this far, there's something special about it. An undefinable quality that makes women want you, and men want to be like you (or vice versa). Either way, you've come too far to turn back, and we promise if you read the rest of this short, two-page intro, you'll either say to yourself, "Hey, that was really worth it" or "There's three minutes of my life I'll never get back." Either way, it's an investment in your future. So, why don't we start with why we wrote this book.

Why we wrote this book
To cash in on the legal music-downloading bonanza brought on by the song-swapping lawsuits of the RIAA (oh rats, did we say that out loud?). I mean, we wrote this book because we really felt that although there are other books out there on iTunes, there was one missing. One that wasn't a hybrid (half Mac, half Windows), one that wasn't 400 pages (iTunes is, after all, designed to be really easy to use), and one that handled things differently—one that tells you just what you need to know to do the cool stuff you want to do in iTunes, and nothing more.

Is this a new concept?
Yes, a book that offers less is definitely a new concept. But in this way, less is more. You see, we feel if you picked up this book, you're probably a lot like us. You want to spend as little time with this book as possible. After all, you didn't buy this book because you want to read. You bought this book because you want to start using iTunes today. The key word here is "using."

Not learning—using. You don't want to learn every single little thing about iTunes (all that freaky stuff like ACC-encoding protocols and how to export your playlists in Unicode format). You just want to create your own custom playlists, learn the most important shortcuts so you don't waste a lot of time, and learn how to make your songs sound good, look good, and play back where you 'em to, whether on a CD, your computer, or your iPod. That's you, or you would've bought one of those 400-page iTunes books, right? Right. So you're not one of them (freaks), you're one of us. We wrote this book for you.

So what makes it different?
It's the format. This isn't a "read it from front to back" book like most other books. Instead, each page in the book covers just one thing. One topic. One idea. One feature. If you want to create a custom EQ for a particular song (say, this one song doesn't have enough bass), turn to page 23 and it will tell you how to do just that. Nothing more. No discussions of room acoustics or debates about analog vs. digital equalizers. Just how to set the EQ for that one song. That's it. One page. One idea. So, turn to the page you have a question about, and you'll get the answer you need. Simple. No info overload.

So where should you start?
Anywhere you want. We organized the book by topic, so you can use it more like a reference manual. For example, if you need to know how to create a Smart Playlist, look in the Table of Contents, in the "Playing with Playlists" chapter. This book is here to help you find the things you're looking for in iTunes for Windows, so just keep it nearby, and at the first sign of "Hmmmm, how do you do that?" just grab the book and the answer is seconds away.

Will I go to jail if I download music from the iTunes Music Store?
Probably. But a good lawyer will have you out in no time. Of course, we're kidding; the whole concept behind the iTunes Music Store is "legal downloading." Besides being 100% legal, it brings good karma (the brewed kind).

Is there much iPod stuff?
Not really. This is really more of an iTunes book (hence the name), but since some of you (the really cool ones) will be downloading an iTunes playlist into an iPod or iPod mini, we wanted to include that part too, so we did. See, we care.

Okay, can we get to it?
I think you've put in enough time here. But before you turn the page and never come back to this introduction again, we want to thank you for having the guts, the courage, the intestinal fortitude to stick it out and read this entire introduction, knowing well beforehand that it was in fact just that—an introduction. You deserve this book. You deserve much more, but all we can give is this book. It's "all we have to give." Now I'm rambling, but you're still here. You are a sport. Seriously though, thanks for giving this new concept, the "less is more" concept, a try. Oh, one more thing: Don't forget to read the chapter intro before each chapter. They're every bit as cohesive, congruent, and critical to your overall understanding as this introduction has been to your understanding of state programs for salmon coastal habitat restoration.

Have fun, play safe, and crank up the jams!

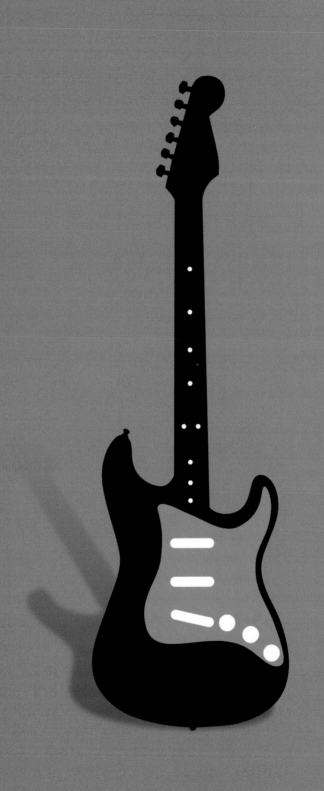

Chapter One

Get the Party Started

iTunes Essentials

Okay, so you just downloaded iTunes for Windows and you're ready to enter a world of digital delights that dare not speak its name. Luckily, that's what this chapter is all about—getting you up and running, movin' and groovin', shakin' and bakin', making no mistakin', etc. Now don't let it mess with your mind that the very first technique in this chapter is "how to play a song." I know, that seems incredibly "duh," but believe it or not, there are people (not you, but other people) who download iTunes, launch it, they see songs in the playlist window, but say (out loud, mind you), "Now what?" We were concerned (and rightly so) that some of these people (you know the type) might buy this book and be totally and utterly stuck on page one unless we included "how to play a song" so we started with that. Now, just because you instinctively knew how to play a song in iTunes (admittedly, it's fairly obvious) doesn't mean you can skip other things in this "essentials" chapter, because there are some cool things that are not as obvious as how to play a song. I can't think of them right off the top of my head, but luckily I remembered to write a bunch of them down, right after this page, so you'll see them in just a minute. Incidentally, it's been a tradition in all our books to name the chapters with a song or movie title (in this case, we chose Pink's "Get the Party Started"), then the actual topic for the chapter appears under that name as a subhead (which in this case is "iTunes Essentials"). Just thought you'd like to know. See, we care.

1

Playing a Song

There's no better place to start than at the beginning. So, let's kick it off with how to play your music files. First, select a song from your Library or a playlist by selecting it with your mouse, then click the play button at the top left of the iTunes window. To speed up the process you can also double-click a song and it will immediately begin playing. You play a song located on a CD in the same way. When you load a music CD into your computer, the album name will appear in the iTunes Source pane. Click the album name to view the album's tracks.

Cool Tip

You can pause a song during play (as long as iTunes is the active window) by pressing the Spacebar on your keyboard. Press the Spacebar again to resume play. Also, try pressing Spacebar when your album name or playlist name is selected in the Source pane. Doing this will begin playing the first track in the list.

Who's Singing the Song?

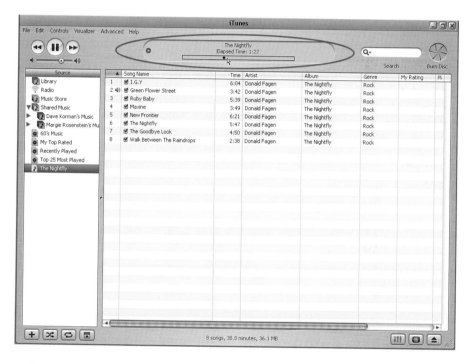

iTunes makes it easy to view a song's info, such as artist's name, song title, total length of the song, elapsed time and so on. It's actually pretty hard to miss. You can view this by looking at the status display. By default, the status display shows the song name and remaining time until the song has finished playing, which is great, but try clicking directly on the song title to switch the view to the artist's name, or click again for album name. Click directly on Remaining Time to toggle through Remaining Time, Elapsed Time, and Total Time the song has played.

Adding Your Own Song Info

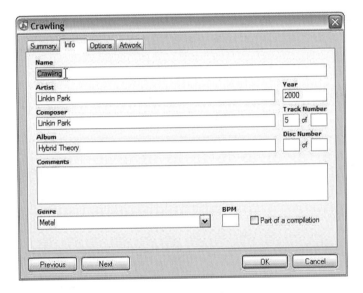

If you want to make several changes to a song at one time, you can't; sorry (kidding). Right-click the song and select Get Info in the shortcut menu. Click the Info tab in the dialog. Here, you'll see the song's Name, Artist, Composer, Album, etc. Make any changes and click OK when finished.

Finding Your Playlist's Total Running Time

If you need the exact total time of the Library or a playlist, glance down at the bottom center of the iTunes window to view the playlist's statistics: song count, play time, and size. Click on the stat line to display the playlist's exact play time in days, hours, minutes, and seconds.

Cool Tip
Be sure to make note of the playlist's total size. This really comes in handy when burning playlists to CDs. This little nugget of info will save you a ton of frustration by allowing you to estimate the total size of your files being copied before you even begin the burning process.

Groovin' with Meters

Try this the next time you're playing a song in iTunes. In the left center of the status display is a small gray circle with a right-facing triangle in the center. Click on this button, and the song's info is replaced by a digital EQ meter. Pretty cool, huh? This serves absolutely no purpose, but it looks pretty cool and kind of zones me out. I guess that's worth something.

Controlling Information Overload

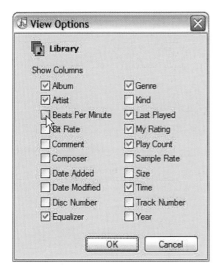

The iTunes Song list window gives you an enormous amount of info–sometimes it can be a bit too much info (especially to new iTunes users). But you don't have to live with this "information overload," because you can tell iTunes which columns you want visible. Press Ctrl-J on your keyboard to display the iTunes View Options dialog. Use this dialog to select which columns you'd like to turn off or on by checking or un-checking options. Once you've made your selections, click OK.

NOTE: Make certain that only the columns you want visible are checked.

Faster Column Views

To get really speedy with columns in iTunes' Song list window, Right-click any column header. Use the shortcut menu that appears to quickly add or remove any column by checking (adding) or unchecking (removing) them.

Changing a Song's Name. Or Artist. Or…

To rename a single field of a song (name, album title, or just about any other info), try this: Click any song to highlight it, then click again directly on the field you want to edit in the Song list window. The field name will become highlighted and editable. Now, type in your changes, press Enter on your keyboard and you're done.

Delete a Song from iTunes

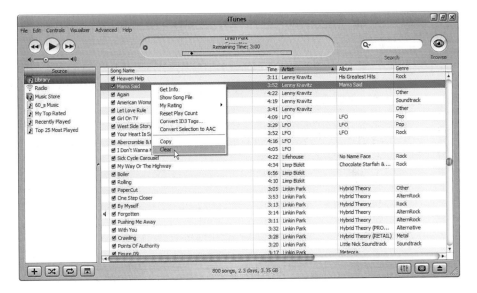

You can quickly and easily delete a song from iTunes by Right-clicking the song's name and selecting Clear in the shortcut menu or by highlighting the song and pressing Delete on your keyboard. And don't sweat accidentally deleting songs; you'll be given a chance to cancel the deletion before iTunes actually removes the song.

Delete Multiple Songs from iTunes

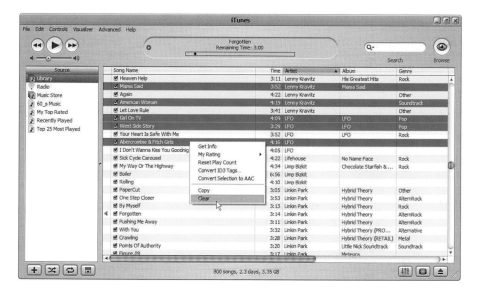

If you'd like to remove several songs at one time, you could delete them individually. But, for those of us who do have lives and would like to get on with 'em, try this instead: Hold the Ctrl key while clicking on the song names that you want to remove. This highlights each song you select. When finished selecting your songs, release the Ctrl key and press Delete on your keyboard.

To select contiguous songs to be deleted, click on the first song, then hold the Shift key. Move your pointer to the last song that you want to select and click it with your mouse, and all files in between are automatically selected. Now, release the Shift key and press Delete on your keyboard.

Rearranging the Song Order

You can very easily rearrange the play order of your songs in iTunes—simply click on the song and drag it to the order you want it to appear—but there are a few catches (gotchas!) to watch out for:

(1) You have to be in a playlist—you cannot change the order of songs in your Library.

(2) To rearrange the order of songs in a playlist, you must have your songs sorted by track number (it's the only blank column header and listed first in the Song list window). You cannot rearrange songs if they are not sorted by track number. Why? I have no idea. It doesn't make sense to me either. Anyway, now you can drag songs into whichever order you'd like.

(3) The last "gotcha" is that you can't rearrange songs if the Shuffle (random play) button is turned on, so make certain that Shuffle is turned off before you try rearranging songs.

User–Friendly Columns

This never fails: The column you want to see is at the far right of your iTunes window and every time you want to view this column, you've got to scroll ALL THE WAY over there, you know, to the right. Well, I hate scrolling (especially to the right)! Really, it's one of my least favorite things, so, I'm not gonna do it. You don't have to do it either. To get your columns up to the front of the line, click-and-hold the column's heading and drag it to the front of the pack or anywhere in between. Repeat this to place your columns in any order you wish.

NOTE: The track number and Song Name columns cannot be moved; they're always listed first and second in the Song list window.

A-to-Z or Z-to-A

Columns are perfect for helping you sort your files and by default are sorted in alphabetical order (A to Z) or numerically (smallest to largest). However, your favorite bands may be White Stripes and U2 and you might even play songs by these bands first every time you open iTunes. I know it's crazy, but there are people like this (you know who you are). iTunes can help. To get to the bottom of your playlist, click on the column's header, which will reverse the sorted order (Z to A and largest to smallest). Now, White Stripes and U2 appear at the top of the playlist.

Finding the Currently Playing Song

iTunes doesn't automatically highlight the song that's currently playing. The first song selected remains highlighted and a little right-facing speaker appears to the left of the song that's actually playing. This is a helpful visual, but the speaker is about the size of a calorie (it's really tiny) and can easily be overlooked, especially when randomly playing songs in a playlist. The next time you're desperately scrolling to find a song that's playing, try pressing Ctrl-L on your keyboard instead. This handy keyboard shortcut instantly jumps you to the playing song.

A Better iTunes Window

Wouldn't it be nice if you could have iTunes resize itself to just the right size—just wide enough to show all of your columns? Well, it can. Just Shift-click on the Maximize/Restore button (in the upper right corner of the iTunes window), and it will resize, fitting every column into view. Shift-click the Maximize/Restore button again to restore your window to its original size.

It's Mini–Tunes

 If you don't need all the info that the screen-hogging iTunes interface offers, you can reduce the size to a much more compact version of iTunes that I call "Mini-tunes." You view the Mini-tunes version of iTunes by clicking once on the Maximize/ Restore button in the upper right corner of the iTunes window, which shrinks iTunes down to just a horizontal bar. Now, drag the bottom right corner of the Mini-tunes window to the left. This hides the status display and leaves only the Rewind, Play, and Fast Forward buttons. (If you feel that iTunes still takes up too much space, then, seriously—it's time to buy a bigger monitor.) Press the Maximize/Restore button to restore iTunes to its original size.

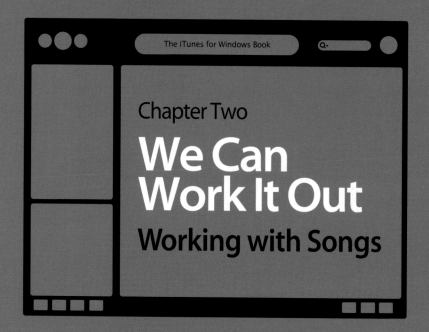

Chapter Two

We Can Work It Out

Working with Songs

See, that's what I was talking about at the end of Chapter One's introduction, when I mentioned that we name chapters with a song title, then the actual description appears below the song. Well, first off, I know what you're thinking—"I don't remember a song named 'We Can Work It Out?'... did Nelly do that, or was it OutKast?" I hate to tell you this, but it was a band that was bigger than both of those (no, it wasn't Linkin Park) but if you really want to know who did the original "We Can Work It Out," you'll have to ask your grandparents—believe me, they'll remember. Of course, you could cheat and go to the iTunes Music Store, type "We Can Work It Out" in the search field, press Enter, and a number of songs named "We Can Work It Out" will appear. Now, as of the writing of this book, the band that actually first made this song famous does not appear in the list of songs, however, this band was so big (even bigger than Bon Jovi, if you can imagine that) that in this list of songs you'll find people who created tribute versions of the song, which was originally written by two young lads from Liverpool (not Liverpool, Ohio, the other Liverpool. In Pennsylvania). Anyway, finding out who did the song in question really won't detract from, or in any way enhance what's really in this chapter, which is all about working with songs once you've brought them into iTunes (and other seemingly important stuff like that).

Pump Up the Volume

There are few things better than being able to control your computer's volume from your keyboard. Okay, there are a lot of better things, but it's still really handy. And fortunately, iTunes makes it easy. Press Ctrl-Up Arrow to crank it, or Ctrl-Down Arrow when the neighbors bang on the wall. Press Ctrl-Alt-Down Arrow to mute iTunes if the cops arrive, and press Ctrl-H to hide your stash before you answer the door (kidding. Kind of).

Stop the Highs and Lows

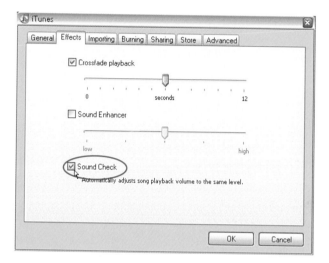

Have you ever had a situation (and I'll bet you have) where you adjusted the volume to the perfect level while playing a song, but the next song came on and was either way too loud, or way too soft? Luckily, iTunes lets you balance the volume between songs with a simple preference setting. Press Ctrl-, (comma) to bring up the iTunes preference dialog then click the Effects tab. Next, select Sound Check to turn on volume leveling. Click OK and (once iTunes determines the volume of each song) all of your songs will play at the same volume.

iTunes' Built-In EQ

iTunes has a built-in graphic equalizer (EQ) for adjusting the audio frequency (the tone quality) of your music to get the best quality sound from your speakers. To view the iTunes EQ, press the EQ button at the bottom right of the iTunes window. Here you can adjust the sliders manually (bass sliders on the left, midrange in the middle, and highs on the right), or use the built-in presets from the pop-up menu found above the sliders.

Saving Your Own Custom EQs

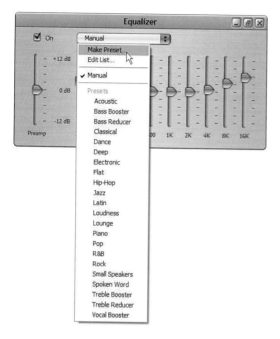

You can also get really geeky and create your own EQ presets. Adjust the EQ's meter manually to create the effect you desire, then choose Make Preset from the top of the built-in presets pop-up menu. You'll be prompted to name your preset. Give it a name and click OK. Now, your custom preset is added to the pop-up menu alphabetically and is there for you to use whenever you'd like.

A Different EQ for Every Song

OK, now you know how to EQ your overall system, but if your playlist contains different genres of music (e.g., R&B, Alternative, Hard Rock, and Dance), you'll find that having just one overall EQ setting just won't cut it. Luckily if you know this little-known tip,
you can set a custom EQ for each song individually. Here's how: Press Ctrl-J to bring up
the View Options dialog, then check Equalizer and click OK. You now have an Equalizer
column added to the right side of your Song list window. Simply click the EQ button
for any song to assign its own EQ setting.

Apply EQ Settings to Groups of Songs

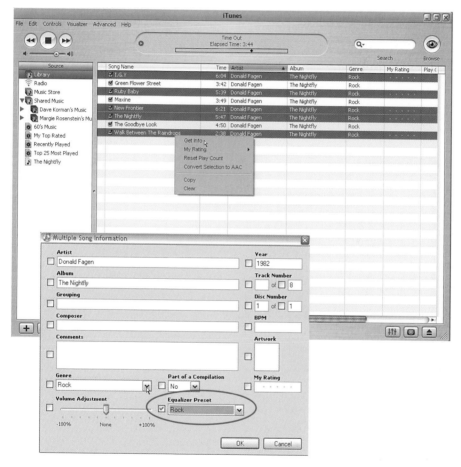

To change the EQ setting for several songs at one time, select your songs by holding the Ctrl (to select non-contiguous songs) or Shift key (to select contiguous songs) to group them. Right-click any selected song and click Get Info in the shortcut menu. (Confirm that you want to edit information for multiple items by selecting Yes.) This opens the Multiple Song Information dialog. Next, click the Equalizer Preset pop-up menu and select an EQ preset, then click OK. Now, all of the selected songs have the same EQ setting. Repeat this as many times as necessary to quickly set the EQ for all songs in a playlist.

You Can Control iTunes from Here

If iTunes is minimized, you don't have to maximize it to use it. I mean, you could, but then we'd mock you for doing it the hard way, because easier is better and there's an easier way. Right-click the iTunes icon in the Taskbar's Notification Area and get all kinds of useful options to control your player. From the shortcut menu you can view the name and artist of the current song. You can also start, stop, shuffle your playlist, and change songs without ever maximizing iTunes.

Add Album Artwork to Your Songs

You can add the artwork from the album the original song came from, but I don't recommend doing this, unless you're retired, or you're in college with a really easy schedule, because once you start—you can't stop. I killed an entire weekend adding album artwork to all my songs, and now when I import a new song, I go searching all over to find the album artwork (much of which is obscure disco club hits from the late 70s and early 80s). Before I tell you how, just remember: I warned you what an intense productivity killer this will become. Start by pressing Ctrl-G (which is the shortcut for "Show Artwork"). Then go to the Web and track down the artwork for your song. You can start at CDNOW.com, or try AllMusic.com. When (if) you find the album cover, just drag it straight from the Web page onto iTunes' Artwork area, and iTunes will automatically scale it down to fit. Now you can kiss your weekend goodbye.

Cool Tip

You can add artwork to several songs at once by pressing Ctrl and clicking each song that you want to add art to. Next, Right-click any selected song and click Get Info on the shortcut menu. Now, drag-and-drop a picture onto the Artwork box. You can also add more than one artwork image to a song by dragging more than one image to the artwork box.

Play It Again and Again and…

By default, each selected song in the iTunes Library or in a playlist will play once then advance to the next song (from top to bottom). You can change this by using several play options. Select the Repeat Playlist/Song button on the bottom left of the iTunes window to cycle through the available options. Click once to replay the entire playlist, click again to continuously replay the currently playing song, or click the button once more to get back to normal and play your playlist only once.

The All On, All Off Shortcut

When selecting or deselecting every song in a playlist, Ctrl-click any song's checkbox, which will instantly select or deselect every song in your playlist. This really comes in handy when burning select songs from your playlists to a CD. For example, you may only want to burn two songs from a playlist containing numerous songs. This allows you to quickly deselect every song in a playlist then choose only the two that you want to actually burn.

Crossfade Between Songs

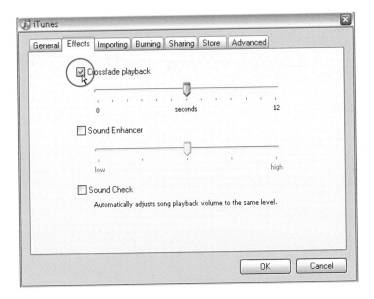

If you're in a big hurry to get through your playlist or just like adding transition effects to your music, try crossfading your songs. Crossfading means that the next song in your playlist begins to play before the current song finishes playing. You hear this effect often on the radio. To add crossfading to your songs, press Ctrl-, (comma) to bring up the iTunes preference dialog, then click the Effects tab. Next, check Crossfade Playback and drag the slider to adjust the length of the Crossfade effect. The higher the number, the longer the crossfade. Press OK and let the crossfading begin!

Adding Songs to Your iTunes Library

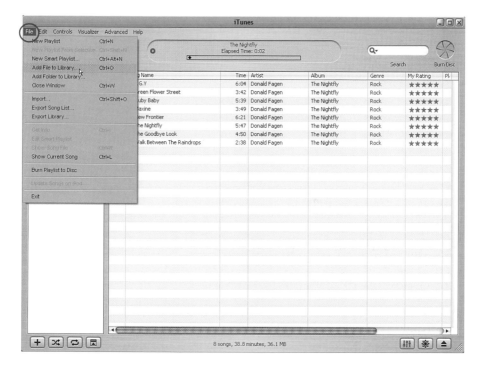

Conveniently, whenever you buy songs from the iTunes Music Store, they're auto-matically added to iTunes. However, songs that you download from other online music providers or songs located in various locations on your hard drive may not be. To manually add songs to iTunes, click File>Add File to Library in the iTunes menu. This opens the Add to Library dialog. Search your hard drive for your files, then click Open to add them to the iTunes Library, or, even better, simply drag-and-drop songs into the iTunes Library's Song list window. That's it! Your song now appears in the iTunes Library.

Chapter Three

Quit Playing Games with My Heart

Playing with Playlists

+ We took a pretty bold step, using a Backstreet Boys song as the title for this chapter. You have to be pretty secure in your music masculinity to even admit you know a Backstreet Boys song, but when you look at the alternative, I think you'll agree we made the right choice. Our other choice for a chapter title was "They're Playing Our Song," which I believe was from a Broadway musical of the same name. So there we were, stuck between a show tune and the Backstreet Boys. Then, after searching the iTunes Music Store, we came up with another song with the term "playing" in the title. It was "Playing for Keeps" by Elvis (as in "The King," not "The Costello"). I was going to go with that, until I heard a preview of the song in iTunes. Now don't get me wrong. I like Elvis probably more than your average guy but I just did not like this particular Elvis song. That doesn't make me a bad person. But the next part does. I went back and listened to the Backstreet Boys' "Quit Playing Games with My Heart" and noticed that my foot was vigorously tapping. Although I would never admit it (even if subpoenaed in a court of law), the next thing I knew, I had popped my *Darren's Dance Grooves* DVD into the player and was learning the same dance steps *NSYNC used in the video ("ain't no lie, baby bye, bye, bye"). Anyway, if you can get past all that, you're about to learn one of the slickest things about iTunes: playlists (in particular, Smart Playlists, and by smart I mean smart enough not to include the Backstreet Boys or show tunes). Kidding!

Create a Playlist

To create a playlist, click File>New Playlist from the iTunes menu or better yet, click the Create Playlist button at the bottom left of the iTunes window. This creates a new playlist ready to be named in the Source pane. Type any name you'd like for your new playlist, press Enter, and you're finished. Now, simply drag-and-drop songs from your Library into your new playlist.

Delete Songs from a Playlist

You've made a mistake, a terrible mistake. You added "Your Kiss Is on My List" by Hall & Oates to your "My Really Cool Songs" playlist (the wife's been adding songs again) and this must be undone and undone quickly. You can delete "Your Kiss Is on My List" by clicking on the song to select it and pressing Delete on your keyboard. You can also Right-click the song title and select Clear from the shortcut menu to delete any song from a playlist. And don't worry—you don't have to hide from your wife—"Your Kiss Is on My List" is safe. You only removed the song from your playlist, not from iTunes.

Delete a Playlist

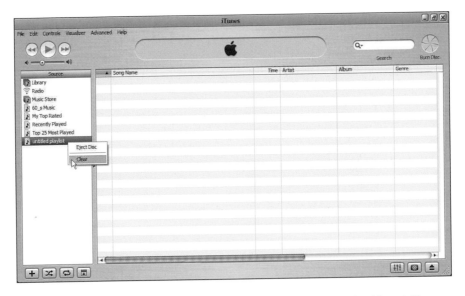

From time to time you're gonna need to delete a playlist and to do this quickly, simply Right-click the playlist's name and select Clear in the shortcut menu. Just make certain that you really want to delete the playlist because you won't be given a chance to cancel this action.

How to Skip over a Song in Your Playlist

Some playlists can get pretty big. I have a couple of playlists that are larger than a lot of "iTuners'" (this is what I call people who use iTunes…I honestly have nothing better to do) entire Library, and I usually don't want to hear every song in a playlist. Well, iTunes lets you skip songs so that you don't have to. To exclude songs from being played in your playlist, uncheck the song by clicking the checkbox next to the song name. Check the song again to add it back to the lineup.

Smart Playlists Really Are Smart

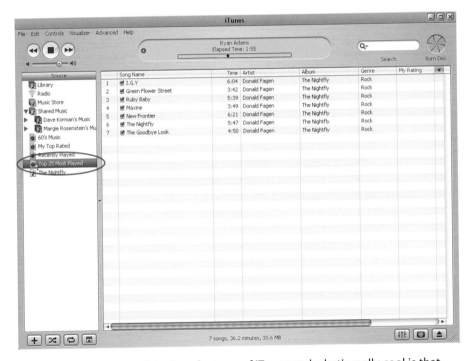

Smart Playlists are one of the best features of iTunes and what's really cool is that they are actually smart. They make sorting and playing your music a breeze. Smart Playlists remember the way that you listen to your music. For example, there are probably 20 or 30 songs out of my entire Library that I play most often. Wouldn't it be great if iTunes remembered, say, my 25 most played songs so that I could quickly and easily get to those songs without having to dig through my Library? Well, iTunes does. Cool, huh? Select the Top 25 Most Played playlist in the Source pane and there they are…your 25 most played songs. Click on the Recently Played playlist to view, well, recently played songs. Select other Smart Playlists to find that iTunes has split up your Library in all kinds of useful ways.

My Top 10, Automatically

Make Smart Playlists work for you by creating a custom Top 10 playlist that auto-matically updates. Choose File and select New Smart Playlist. This opens the Smart Playlist dialog. In the first pop-up menu, choose Play Count; from the second menu, choose Is Greater Than and then type "5" in the info field. Enter 10 in the Limit To field (so you'll only wind up with 10 songs—your top 10) and in the Selected By field, select Most Often Played. Also make certain that Live Updating is checked. Click OK and you'll have a new playlist made up of your top 10 most played songs, in the order you most play them, and it's updated automatically.

Shortcut for Creating Smart Playlists

Clicking on the Create Playlist button at the bottom left of the iTunes window lets you create new playlists, but if you hold the Shift key, you'll notice that the button changes to a "gear" icon, giving you a quick way to create a Smart Playlist instead.

Create a Playlist from a Selection

Here's a handy tip for creating a playlist from selected songs. Start by selecting the song or songs from your Library that you want to add to a new playlist, then click File>New Playlist From Selection in the iTunes menu. Your new playlist is instantly created (and ready to be named) containing the selected songs.

Everybody's a Critic: Rating Songs

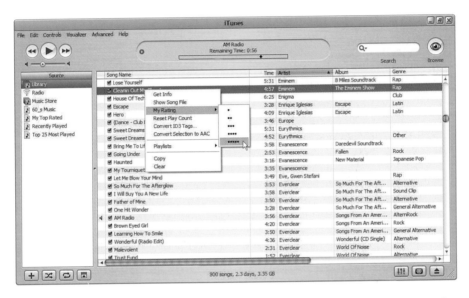

There's really only one good use for rating songs, and that's to rate your songs with five stars. Honestly, how many of you take the time to rate your songs with one, two, or even three stars? If it's a one-, two-, or three-star song, it's just not worth the effort. But rating your songs is very useful for allowing you to quickly sort your favorite songs. To rate a song, select it by Right-clicking it and pointing to My Rating in the shortcut menu. Now, click a rating (one to five stars).

Cool Tip
You can also rate your songs by first selecting a song, then clicking in the My Rating column in the Song list window and dragging your pointer left to right to scroll the one- to five-star rating.

A Five–Star Playlist

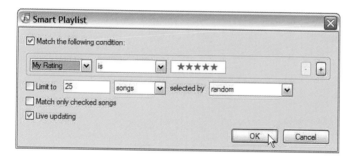

By using your Smart Playlist dialog, you're just one click away from having iTunes create a playlist of just your five-star-rated songs. Here's how: Go under iTunes' File menu and choose New Smart Playlist. Then in the Smart Playlist dialog, change the first pop-up menu to "My Rating." The second pop-up menu will automatically change to "is" and the info field will show five rating stars. Click OK and a new play-list will appear in your playlist column (ready for you to name) made up of nothing but your five-star-rated songs.

A Window of Its Own

If you'd like to have multiple playlists open at one time, or if you'd just like to have your playlist open in a separate window, double-click directly on a playlist's icon in the Source pane. This opens a new window for only that playlist.

Reset a Song's Play Count

iTunes automatically keeps a record of how many times you play each song. And I'm certain this is useful for some reason (as soon as I find that reason I'll share it with you). But who knows, maybe you already have a use for it. Well, if you do, you can view this info by looking at the Play Count column in the iTunes Song list window. Well, you might just be a little embarrassed to actually see that you've played "Dancing Queen" by Abba over 100 times in the past month. So, to hide your shame, you can quickly reset a song's play count by Right-clicking on the song and choosing Reset Play Count in the shortcut menu. I bet you're already feeling better.

Combine Playlists

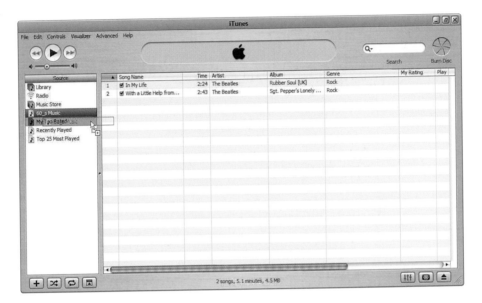

OK, you've created 20 or 30 playlists and realized that you could have actually combined your "Jazz" and "Blues" playlists. Well, you can quickly combine playlists by dragging-and-dropping them onto one another. Try this: Click-and-drag a playlist onto another playlist that you created. Open the playlist. You'll now see the songs from both playlists combined. This doesn't delete the playlist that you dragged; it only places the contents of one playlist into another. If you no longer need one of the combined playlists, simply delete it.

NOTE: You can't drag-and-drop playlists onto iTunes' default Smart Playlists or Smart Playlists that you create.

Exporting Your Playlists

When burning CDs, you're almost always going to want to print some type of CD cover. You know, something to tell you the song names, song order, album, genre, and so on. Well, the easiest way to do this is by exporting your playlist's info. To do this, Right-click your playlist in the Source pane and select Export Song List in the shortcut menu. Choose a location on your hard drive to save the file and click Save. iTunes saves your playlist as a tab-delimited text file. Now, use your favorite spreadsheet or database program such as Excel, Access, or FileMaker to open and edit the file.

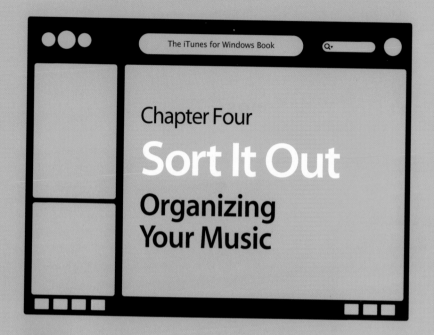

Chapter Four

Sort It Out

Organizing Your Music

Okay, this song is perhaps a bit obscure, but "Sort It Out" is a real song recorded by not just one, but four different groups (we chose the Twelve Caesars' version, if it matters). By the way, if you search for "Twelve Caesars" in the iTunes Music Store, you'll find an audio book called *The Twelve Caesars*, but needless to say it doesn't contain the song "Sort It Out." Shame. Anyway, we thought the ultimate song for this chapter's title was simply "Organize." I know you're thinking "Oh, right—there's a song named 'Organize.' Oh yeah, I believe that." Well, my skeptical friend, believe it—it's called "Organize" and it's by Little Steven and the Disciples of Soul (yes, *that* Little Steven of Bruce Springsteen and HBO's *Sopranos* fame). We thought "It's right on the money, but it's too short," so we kept searching for the ultimate song name for this chapter. Since this chapter is all about organizing, sorting, and generally keeping track of your music in iTunes, we thought we might get away with a derivative term, like "sort" rather than organize. That's when we found "Sort It Out." Once we learned that not only did the Twelve Caesars record a song by that name, but also Polara, Sixth Sense Atmosphere, and Brenda Freed (who even named her album "Sort It Out"), we were sold—"Sort It Out" it is. Hey, we spent a lot of time on the title, because organizing is a very important chapter, which will become more and more important the more you use iTunes and the more songs you add to your collection. Hey, that last sentence actually made some sense. Let's edit it out.

Can't Find Your Songs?

Don't feel stupid because you can't find your songs. There are a lot of song-location-challenged people out there. Apple knew this; that's why they included a search feature in iTunes. Actually, using iTunes' search is much faster than scrolling through thousands of songs in your Library. To perform a song search, begin typing the song title, album title, artist, or genre in the search window. iTunes narrows your search as you type and displays fewer and fewer results until you find just what you're looking for.

NOTE: To display your entire Library or playlist again, simply delete the text from the search window or click the X button in the right corner of the search window.

Browsing Is a Breeze

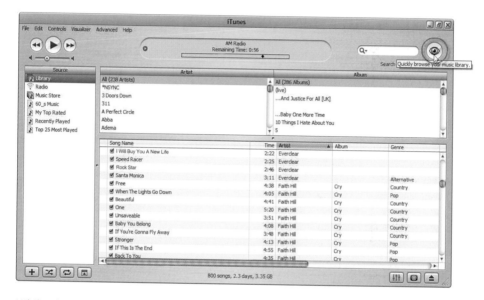

While playlists are great for sorting your various types of music, they take time to set up. Well, what do you do in a pinch, when you need a playlist in a hurry? Click the Browse button! Browse is like playlists on steroids. Using Browse, you can very quickly sort your music by Artist and Album. So, if you're in the mood for nothing but Blink 182, you can have your Song list display just their tunes.

To use this, first you must be in the iTunes Library (the Browse button does not appear when viewing playlists). Now, click the Browse button in the upper right corner of the iTunes window. When you click the Browse button, rather than giving you a long scrolling list view of all the songs in your library, it gives you something more like the column view of an Explorer window, with different category panes sorted by info you've entered (or which was embedded) in your music files. Select any Artist or Album listed to display all related music in your Library.

Browsing by Genre

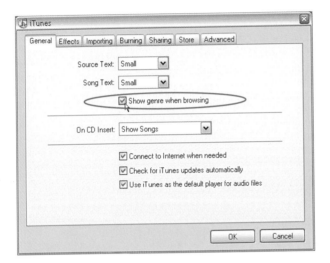

You can also browse your music by genre. This really comes in handy if you're in the mood for Japanese Pop (actual genre; scary, huh?). To add genre to your browse window, press Ctrl-, (comma) to open the preference dialog. On the General tab, check Show Genre When Browsing, then click OK. The genre pane now appears in the iTunes browse window. And, you're just one click away from quickly viewing all of your Japanese Pop songs (still scary).

Bring Order to iTunes

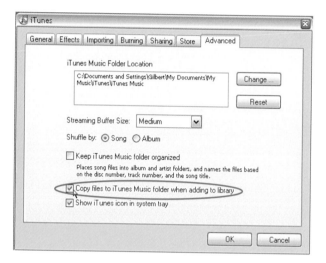

When you play a song that's on your hard drive but not located in your iTunes music folder, iTunes simply creates a shortcut to the original song file and places that shortcut in your iTunes music folder. So basically, the original songs can be scattered all over your hard drive, in different folders. However, if you want to bring some order to your music world, iTunes can instead copy the songs into your iTunes folder (rather than just making shortcuts), keeping all your original song files organized in one central location. To do this, press Ctrl-, (comma) to open the preference dialog. Next, click the Advanced tab and check Copy Files to iTunes Music Folder When Adding to Library, then click OK.

Come Together

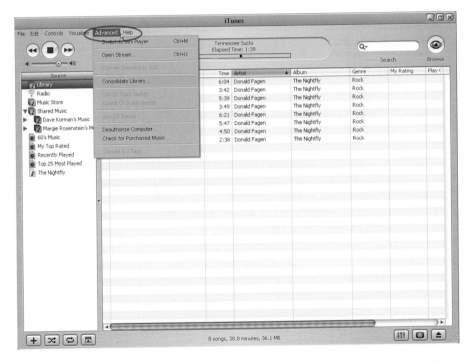

If you're like me, your songs are located in a dozen different places on your hard drive. Well, you can bring instant order to your music collection by selecting Advanced> Consolidate Library in the iTunes menu. This action copies all of your audio files from their various locations into your iTunes music folder, bringing an eerie sense of peace to your high-tech world.

Add Custom and Multiple Genres

Believe it or not, you may actually have songs that don't quite fit into any of iTunes' preset genres. I know, it's hard to imagine—there are a ton of presets. But, you can add custom genres to your songs or even add multiple genres to a song. Here's how: Right-click on your song and select Get Info in the shortcut menu. This opens the Song Information dialog. Next, click the Info tab and select Custom from the Genre pop-up menu. Now, type any name you wish to call its genre and click OK. To add multiple genres, simply type the genre names separated by a comma (for example, "Rock, Hard Rock, Metal").

NOTE: Adding more than one genre to your songs allows you to display them in multiple categories when browsing or searching your Library.

Font Super-Sizing

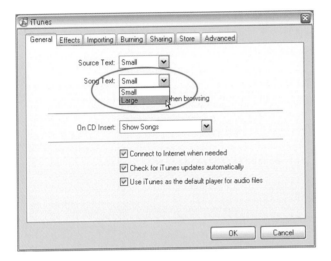

If the font in the iTunes song list appears too small to you, then your eyes are bad and you need to get glasses. Or, you could just increase iTunes' font size. That'll work too. You can do this by pressing Ctrl-, (comma) to open the preference dialog, and then clicking on the General tab. Select Large from the Song Text pop-up menu, then click OK. Now if the text is still too small, you probably are going blind and really do need glasses.

Get to the Good Stuff:
Editing Out Long, Boring Intros

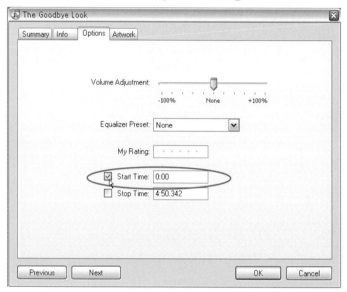

If you've got a song with a way too long intro (like the incredibly long intro to Aldo Nova's "Fantasy", an otherwise way-cool song), you can trim away that intro and get right to the "good stuff" using iTunes. You start by finding out exactly when the "good stuff" starts (look up top for the time display), then Right-click on the song in your playlist and click Get Info in the shortcut menu. When the Info window appears, click on the Options tab. You'll see a field for Start Time. Check the Start Time check-box, enter the time when the good stuff starts (for "Fantasy" it's 1:04), and you're set—the way too long intro is long gone.

Editing a Bunch of Songs at Once

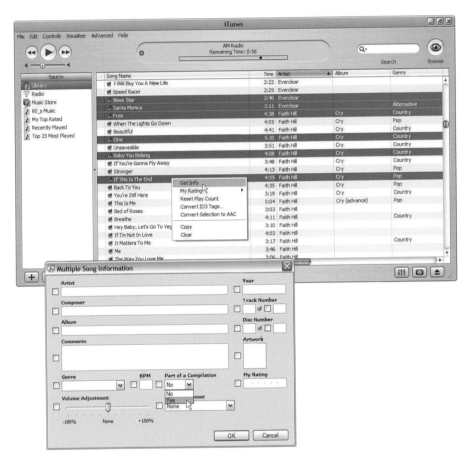

Earlier we showed how to edit an individual song's info, but what do you do if you need to edit several songs using the same information? For instance, you have several songs from an album for which you want to change the Genre from Rock to Hard Rock. Try this: Select the songs that you want to change. Right-click on any selected song and select Get Info in the shortcut menu. Now, use the Multiple Song Information dialog to enter whatever information you want to make the same. Click OK when finished and your changes are applied to each of the selected songs.

Quick Ratings

If you're playing a song and decide you want to rate it, just Right-click the iTunes icon in the Taskbar's Notification Area, point to My Rating in the shortcut menu, and click a rating. It doesn't get much easier or faster than that!

Locate Your Songs

Do you ever wonder where your songs are located on your hard drive? Not me, personally I couldn't care less; I need a little mystery in my life. But if your life's already exciting enough then you can quickly locate a song by Right-clicking on it in the Song list window and selecting Show Song File in the shortcut menu. This opens the song's folder in an Explorer window showing its exact location on your hard drive.

Chapter Five

Can't Buy a Thrill

The iTunes Music Store

This chapter title is a bit misleading, because it makes it sound like downloading music from the iTunes music store isn't thrilling. It's fun, it's sometimes exciting (like when you come across that song that you haven't heard in years, and couldn't remember the name of, but there it is and you can buy it right this second), but I'm not sure thrilling is really the right adjective. Now, I'll tell you what's thrilling: the exact moment when my wife opens the American Express bill and she gets to the charges from Apple Computer for music downloads. That part has some real thrills. It's sometimes accompanied by the sound of smashing glass, shrieks of horror, and shortly thereafter the faint sounds of sirens, which grow louder and louder by the minute. Now that, my friends, is thrilling. So you really can buy a thrill, for around 99¢. As thrilling as "bill day" at my house is, this may not be true, but I'm sure there's somebody out there who gets it worse than I do. During a speech about the success of the iTunes Music Store, Apple's CEO, Steve Jobs, answered a question that was probably on the minds of many in the crowd: Who has spent the most money buying songs from the iTunes Music Store? Of course, for personal privacy reasons he didn't give the person's name (probably Bill Gates), but he did mention that the iTunes Music Store's #1 customer had already spent more than $29,000 downloading songs. If it, indeed, was a man, and if, indeed, he's lucky enough to still have a wife, I'm pretty certain the next sound he heard was that of a cast-iron frying pan at close range. Repeatedly.

My iTunes Music Store Wish List

Wouldn't it be great if the iTunes Music Store offered a "wish list" feature (like Amazon.com)? I'm always finding music that interests me, but I need a little time to think about my purchase before dropping 99¢. The iTunes Music Store is 99¢-ing me to death. Anyway, here's a little trick that will let you create your own "wish list" of music that you can revisit at any time.

Start by creating a new folder on your desktop called "iTunes Wish List" or whatever. Then when you're browsing through the Music Store and find a song (or album) you think you might want later, just click-and-drag the song's album into your "Wish List" folder on your desktop. The URL is saved in your folder and now you're just a click away from the album's page in the iTunes Music Store.

iTunes on a Budget

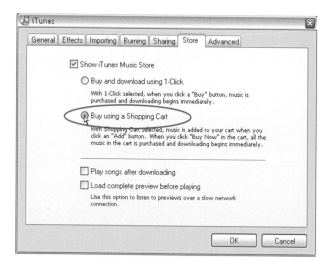

My wife no longer allows me to use the Buy And Download Using 1-Click feature of the iTunes Music Store (hey, it's easy to get carried away with one-click downloads for only 99¢ a pop). If you're like me and have no sense of how quickly 99¢ here and 99¢ there adds up, then you might want to turn on the iTunes Shopping Cart feature, which puts all of your music selections into one shopping cart (rather than instantly downloading and charging as you go). This way, you can see a list of all your songs before you buy, and give yourself a chance to make certain that you didn't get a little carried away.

To do this, press Ctrl-, (comma) to open the preference dialog and click on the Store tab. Then choose Buy Using a Shopping Cart. Now, when you're shopping, the Buy Song button becomes the Add Song button. Your songs aren't downloaded or charged until you select the Buy Now button when checking out.

Tell a Friend

Did you find a song that you really like? Do you want to tell a friend about it? Well, that's really thoughtful, and fortunately, being thoughtful and sending your friend a link to the song in the iTunes Music Store is easy. Simply click-and-drag the song title or album cover to a new message window in Outlook or Outlook Express. The song's URL is automatically pasted into the message and ready to send to your friend. And when your friend clicks on the URL, it will open their iTunes player and take them to the song in the Music Store. And, again, thanks for being so thoughtful…no really, that's a nice thing you've done.

Better Song Previews for Dial-Up Users

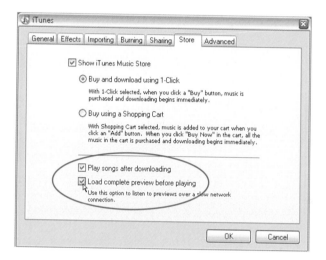

If you have a dial-up connection to the Internet then you already know what an enormous pain it is to try to listen to streaming audio (or streaming anything) on the Internet. Well, song previews from the iTunes Music Store are exactly those…audio streams. Fortunately, there is something that you can do to eliminate choppy, garbled, and incomprehensible music previews. Don't stream them. Instead, press Ctrl-, (comma) to open the iTunes preference dialog, click the Store tab, then check Play Songs After Downloading and Load Complete Preview Before Playing at the bottom of the dialog. Click OK. Now, your songs and previews will download completely before beginning to play.

"Deauthorize" Your Computer

When you purchase songs from the iTunes Music Store, you're authorized to listen to them on up to three computers that are associated with your iTunes account. Basically, this means that you can only listen to the songs you purchase on three computers at any given time (this is meant to assist in preventing illegal sharing of music). Whichever computer you originally used to download your songs to is automatically authorized to play the songs you purchased. You can authorize up to two more computers (perhaps your laptop and office computer) to also play your songs. You cannot play your songs on a different (fourth) computer until you deauthorize one of the three. You authorize or deauthorize your computer by clicking Advanced>Authorize Computer, or Advanced>Deauthorize Computer in the iTunes menu.

Linking to Songs in the Store from Your Webpage

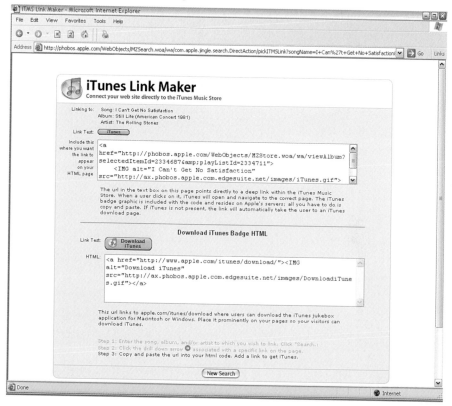

If you've got a website and want to send users directly to a particular song in the ITMS, Apple is happy to help. In fact, they'll even generate the HTML code for you so all you have to do is copy that code onto your webpage. It's called the "iTunes Link Maker" and you reach it by launching your Web browser and going to www.apple.com/itunes/linkmaker. There you'll find search fields by song, album, and artist name. Enter the info for the song you're looking for, and if it's available on the ITMS, a new screen will appear with your HTML code, ready for copying and pasting.

Spoiling Your Kids...Automatically

If you're rich, and have children, you're going to love this tip. You can set up the ITMS to give your kids an iTunes allowance (you can fund this from their trust fund) and each month money will be automatically deposited into their ITMS account. How does this help you? Well, since you're not giving them a credit card, you don't have to worry about them abusing it. Because it's an allowance, they can't spend more than you give them, and it keeps your butler from having to drive a check over to their dorm room. Here's how to set up their allowance: At the home page of the ITMS, click on the word Allowance on the left-hand side to bring up the Set Up an iTunes Allowance page. You can then choose to give your child up to $200 a month in an ITMS allowance. If you choose $200, Apple automatically sends an email to a local therapist and schedules an appointment for you, because clearly you need to have your head examined. Once you've entered your information, click Buy Now and Apple will ask you to sign in to your account.

Music Preview Shortcut

If you're searching for a particular song and about 14 different versions by 8 different artists appear, you'll love this tip. To quickly hear a preview of each song, start by double-clicking the first song in the list. Then, as soon as you realize it's not the right version, just press the right arrow key on your keyboard, and it will stop playing the previous song and start playing the next song down. Try this once and you'll use it again and again.

The Shortcut to Finding More of an Artist's Work

The next time you do a search, when the results appear, look in the Artist column. You'll see a little gray circle with a right-facing arrow that appears immediately after the artist's name. This is a super-shortcut to more of that particular artist's work. Click on it, and a page of nothing but their work appears. Pretty darn handy.

The ITMS's Hidden Links

If you see text in the top section of the iTunes Music Store, chances are it's a live clickable link that will take you directly to a song, an artist, a genre, etc. How do you know which bits of text are live links? Just move your cursor over the text and if it underlines, you can click it. (You can even click on the Explicit warning, and it will take you to a detailed description of just what explicit means. Just in case you were wondering, it means "really naughty stuff.")

What to Do If the "Buy Now" Button Says "Add Song"

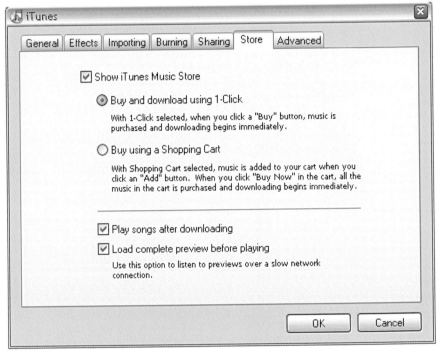

This one trips up quite a few people. It's been a week or so since you last shopped in the ITMS, and you go to buy a song but the button that used to say "Buy Song" now says "Add Song." If this happens to you, you need to reinstall Windows XP. (Kidding. Just a joke.) Actually, what this means is that you (or someone using your machine) must have turned on the iTunes Music Store's Shopping Cart function, which lets you add songs to a cart then check out and buy all your songs at once, rather than buying them song by song (which is the default setting). To get back to the "one-click" brand of shopping, go under the iTunes Preferences, click on the Store icon, then choose Buy and Download Using 1-Click and click OK. Your all-too-familiar Buy Song button will be back at work, ready to make your music collection surge.

The Home Page Navigation Dots

On the ITMS home page there are five horizontal rows of CDs that appear with tiny thumbnail covers. There are blue navigation arrows on the end of each row so you can see other CDs in a horizontally scrolling list, and that's what most people use to navigate, but there's a shortcut. See those four little circles in the top center of each row? Those not only show you where you are in the horizontal scrolling list, they're also clickable, so if you want to go to the third set of CDs, you don't have to keep clicking the blue buttons—just click the third circle from the left.

Ready for a "Power Search"?

Most of the time, the standand ITMS search field works just fine, but if you want more control over your search, you need to do a Power Search. To do a Power Search, click and hold the little magnifying glass icon that appears on the left side of the standard Search field. Choose Power Search from the pop-up list that appears. This brings up a special search dialog across the top of the ITMS where you can search by multiple fields including Song, Artist, Album, Genre, and Composer.

Find an Artist's Website

If an artist is featured on the ITMS site (we don't mean they just have songs on there for download, we mean they've got their own special feature area, with large graphics and a complete discography), many times you'll find a direct link to the artist's own website right on that page. Click the link, usually called (big shock here) "Website," and it'll launch your Web browser and take you to their site. Fairly handy.

Don't Use the Back Button. Shortcut It.

If you want to return to your previous ITMS page, you don't have to travel up to the "Back Button" (the black left-arrow button). Instead, just press Control-[(left bracket) and your hands never leave the keyboard.

Don't Just Search: Browse

If you prefer searching by Genre (like all Opera songs or all Hip Hop), just click the Browse button in the top right-hand corner of iTunes, and instead of browsing the songs on your hard drive, it will let you browse, by genre, the songs in the iTunes Music Store. You click on the Genre, it'll bring up a list of artists; then you click on the Artist, and it'll give you a list of their available songs. Not a bad way to spend the day.

Sort Your Searches

Once you've done a search and the results appear in the main window, you can re-sort the results in the order you want them by clicking the column names. By default all your searches are sorted by Relevance. However, if you prefer to have the results listed alphabetically by artist, then just click the Artist column header and they'll be instantly re-sorted. See, it's all about you, isn't it?

Keep Other People from Buying on Your Computer

If you're using ITMS at work (and good for you if you are), then you'll probably want to protect yourself while you've stepped away for lunch, for a break, or to steal some paper clips. Just because you're stealing doesn't mean it's OK for others, so before you sneak back to the supply room, click on the Account button at the top right of the ITMS. A dialog will appear where you can click Sign Out, and then the ability to buy songs is turned off until you sign on again. And with the money you'll make from selling those office supplies on eBay, it won't be long before you'll be logged on again and downloading songs during an important meeting.

How Much Have You Bought?

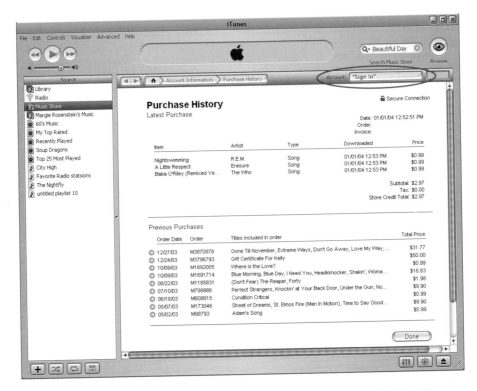

If you're wondering, "Just how much have I spent at the iTunes Music Store?" I believe Apple knows, but you can find out just as easily. Once you're logged in to the Music Store, click on the Account button in the upper right-hand corner of the ITMS. Even though you're already logged in, it will prompt you for your password. Enter it and click the View Account button. When your account info page appears, click the Purchase History button and hang on to your hat, as every purchase you've made (and what they cost) appears neatly in a row. A long row.

Can't Remember Which Songs Were Hot That Year?

Don't worry… just look it up on Billboard's Hot 100 chart! Don't subscribe to Billboard? Don't sweat it—you can access the Hot 100 songs (and buy them) right from within the iTunes Music Store. In the list of categories on the left side of the music store, click on Charts. This takes you to a listing of charts and there you'll find the Billboard Hot 100. Click on it, and a list will appear to the right with all years listed. Just click on a year and the Hot 100 list for that year will appear in your main window, making you feel incredibly old.

If You're Sharing Music, They Won't Hear ITMS-Downloaded Songs

If you've got your iTunes set up for sharing over a network, iTunes doesn't let the people sharing your music hear the songs you bought and downloaded from the ITMS—it just skips right over them in the playlist. Why? Because their machines are not authorized as approved computers for sharing your legally downloaded songs (for copyright protection purposes). So how do you let them hear your purchased music over your network? There's only one way—make their computer one of the three authorized computers, which you're probably unlikely to do, so in short, they're out of luck.

Getting Faster ITMS Song Previews

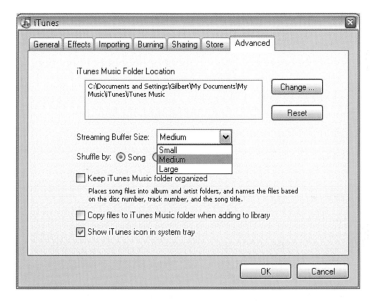

If you've got a high-speed Internet connection, you can have faster loading of both ITMS previews and music shared over a network by tweaking one little preference setting. Go under iTunes preferences and click on the Advanced icon. You'll see a pop-up menu for Streaming Buffer Size. By default it's set to Medium, but if you have a high-speed Internet connection, you can change this to Small, which will load previews and shared songs even faster because now it's buffering a smaller amount of data before it's played.

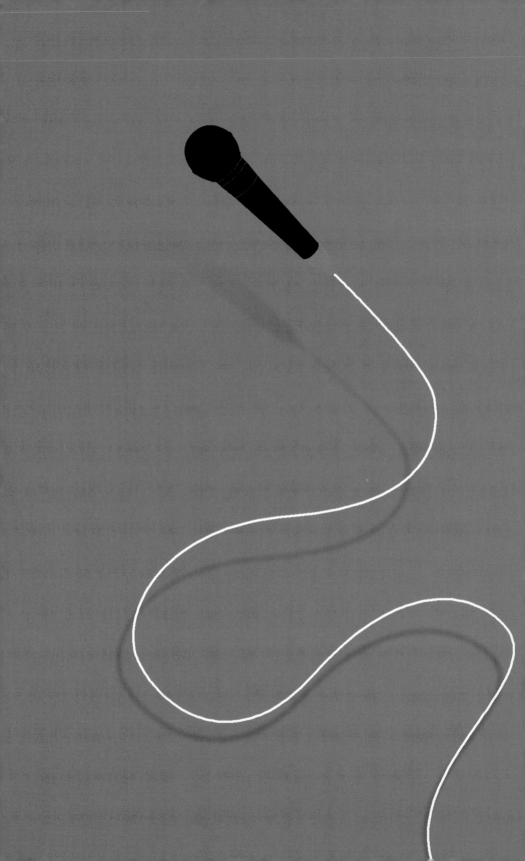

Chapter Six

Rip It Up

Importing from CDs and Burning Your Own CDs

We did find a better song title than "Rip It Up" (Rip being a nod to the term "ripping" which is iTunes lingo for importing a song from a CD). In fact, we found the perfect title: "Rip Session" by M?K (looks like a typo; it's not), from his album "Da Question Mark" which I found by searching in the iTunes Music Store. So why didn't we use that title? The song is…well…naughty. At least, it has some naughty words. How do I know? Well, first the iTunes Music Store gives you a warning that a song contains explicit lyrics (it says in red capital letters "EXPLICIT"). But ya know, we needed to know just how explicit , because the title of that song is perfect. So, seeing as we're adults clearly over the age of 21, we double-clicked the preview and son-of-a-gun they were right. The first two words pretty much garnered the song the "Explicit" tag. I suspect some people will stop the song dead in its tracks because of its sheer explicit explicitness (at least that's what we did). But after we giggled for a minute (because it was so naughty right off the bat), for the sake of our research, we played the rest of the preview. Wow, that is one naughty song. There are words in there I didn't even say when I tripped and slammed my knee right into the corner of a coffee table. Here's the bad part: Even though we didn't use "Rip Session" as the title for this chapter about importing music from CDs, you know and I know you're going straight to the iTunes Music Store, you're going to search for "Rip Session" and double-click on it to hear the preview. Hey, don't say we didn't warn ya.

Taggin' Your MP3s

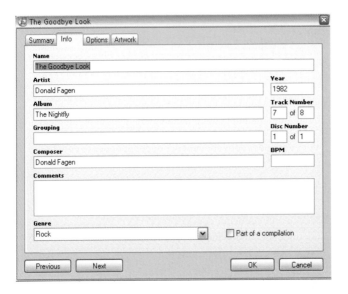

This is just a reminder that all of the song info for your iTunes music is stored in the song's Info dialog, and if you download MP3s from the Web, you already know how often song names, artists, and album information are shockingly incorrect. Well, you can edit an MP3's tags in the same way you do any iTunes-purchased or CD-imported songs by Right-clicking a song in your list and clicking Get Info in the shortcut menu. Click the Info tab in the dialog and here you can type in the correct name and fix any other horribly wrong or misspelled info you want.

Quick Tag Edits for Multiple Songs

Earlier, we showed you how to make changes to a song's tag information, but you can also quickly edit the tag information for multiple songs without ever leaving the Info tab of the preference dialog. To do this, Right-click any song and select Get Info in the shortcut menu. Next, click the info tab and you can jump back and forth to songs in your song list by clicking the Previous and Next buttons located at the bottom of the Info tab's window. Clicking Previous or Next jumps you to, well, the previous or next song in the lineup.

Auto Tags

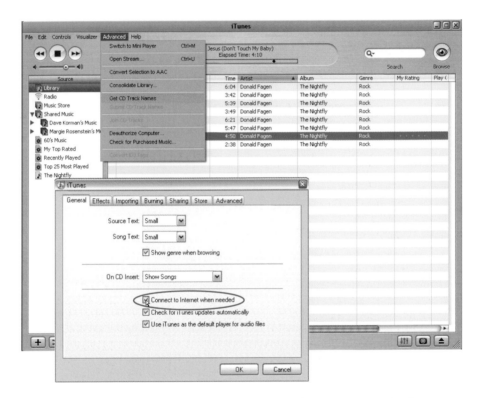

If entering a song's tag information isn't exactly your favorite thing to do, then you may not have to. You can have iTunes automatically go to the Web, search for the song info (in the CDDB Internet audio database), and enter it into the song's tag information field for you (pretty cool, huh?). There are only two catches: (1) You can only do this when you're importing songs from an audio CD, and (2) you must have an active Internet connection.

You can set up iTunes to do this automatic search by pressing Ctrl-, (comma) to open the iTunes preference dialog. Click the General tab, click the checkbox for Connect To Internet When Needed, then click OK. Now when you're importing a CD, click Advanced>Get CD Track Names in the iTunes menu and it'll do its Internet thing.

CD–Quality Importing

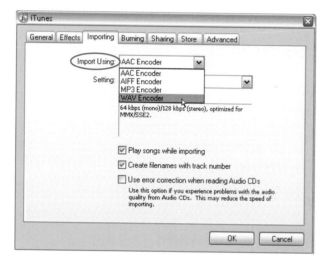

The MP3 format has revolutionized music on the Internet, and while MP3 is a great format for compressing and reducing the size of audio files, there is a trade-off—smaller file sizes mean a loss of quality due to the file's compression. And, although MP3 is the Web standard, when you're importing songs from a CD, you're not on the Web, so you can use a higher quality format that gives you a much "closer to CD quality" audio encoding than MP3 provides. It's called AAC encoding. You turn on AAC encoding by pressing Ctrl-, (comma) to open the preference dialog then choosing the Importing tab. Next, select AIFF or WAV Encoder from the Import Using pop-up menu. Now all your songs imported from CDs will use the highest quality encoding.

Import Your Way

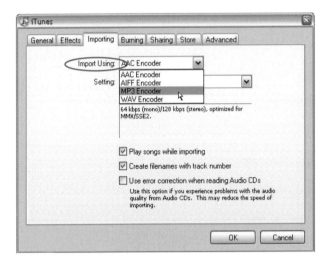

You don't have to import your music the way that iTunes thinks you should; you actually have several available options that allow you almost total control over how you import. Press Ctrl-, (comma) to open the preference dialog, then click on the Importing tab. Here you can see the various import options that are available. Use the Import Using pop-up to select which format you want to use when importing music. AIFF (standard Mac audio format) and WAV (standard Windows audio format) import exact copies of your music, without compression. If you plan on putting your music on an iPod then you may want to import your songs as MP3s. Use the Setting pop-up to adjust the quality of imported music.

NOTE: Importing audio in an AIFF or WAV format saves your songs in the largest possible size and highest possible quality. MP3 format compresses your files, making them smaller and allowing them to be more easily stored on players and your computer.

Eliminate the Gaps...Join the Tracks

There may be cases when you don't want there to be a gap between tracks. For example, let's say you're importing songs from *Boston's Greatest Hits*, and although the song "Long Time" was released as a single, on the album there's a pre-song called (aptly enough) "Foreplay." These two songs are really "one big song" with just a brief moment of silence between them. However, when you import the tracks into iTunes, they import as two separate tracks with a big gap in between, ruining an important moment in classic rock history. To prevent this from happening, you can join the two tracks before you import them. To do this, Ctrl-click both tracks to select them, then click Advanced>Join CD Tracks in the iTunes menu. A small join bracket will appear, linking the two songs. Now the tracks will import as one song. Later, if you decide that "Foreplay" and "Long Time" should be two separate songs, you can choose Unjoin CD Tracks from the Advanced menu.

NOTE: You cannot join tracks that have already been imported into iTunes.

Auto-Import Your Music

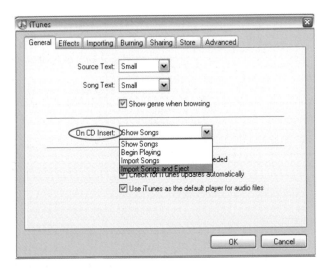

By default, iTunes displays the contents of a music CD when you load it into your computer, which is nice; however, you can change the way iTunes handles your CDs to make it downright helpful. For example, say you're importing your entire collection of music CDs. Well, you can set up iTunes to automatically import your music instead of just showing the CD's contents. That would speed up the process, huh? Here's how: Press Ctrl-, (comma) to open the preference dialog. Next, click the General tab and next to the pop-up that reads On CD Insert, change Show Songs to Import Songs and Eject. Now when you insert a music CD, iTunes will automatically import all the songs and eject the disc so you can pop in the next one.

Import to Playlists

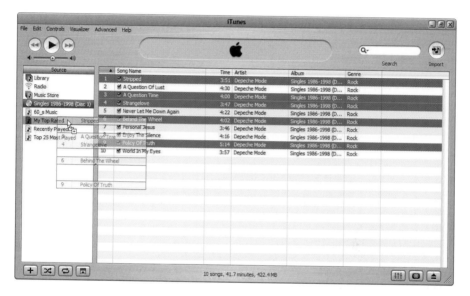

Here's another timesaving import tip. You don't have to necessarily import songs from a CD into your Library before you add them to your playlists. Instead, simply drag-and-drop your songs from the CD Song list window into any playlist. This automatically imports your song into that playlist (with the original appearing in the Library automatically).

<table>
<tr><td>Cool Tip</td></tr>
</table>

You can follow the same steps to conveniently place music files located anywhere on your hard drive into the playlists of your choice.

Damaged CD? iTunes Can Help

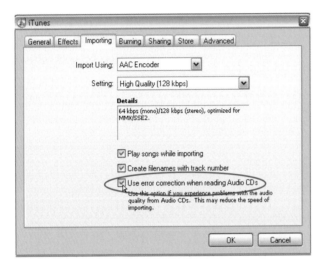

If you've found your cat using the CD that you were about to import into iTunes as a chew toy, don't toss it in the trash just yet. iTunes can sometimes help import scratched and otherwise traumatized CDs. Press Ctrl-, (comma) to open the preference dialog and click the Importing tab. Next, check Use Error Correction When Reading Audio CDs and click OK. Now when you import the scratched CD, iTunes will try to eliminate any errors by importing at a higher quality and using a slower method of importing.

One-Button Burning

You've spent days, hours, or maybe weeks importing your music into iTunes and putting together your playlists, and now it's time to start burning your songs to CD. After all, that's the beauty of digital music...you can take it with you. To burn a CD in iTunes, select the playlist that you want to copy, then click the Burn Disc button located at the top right of the iTunes window (the Burn Disc button only appears when viewing a playlist). iTunes will ask you to insert a blank disc (if you haven't already) and opens your computer's CD tray. Insert your disc, close the tray and iTunes will display the song count and total play time of the songs being copied, and prompt you to once again click Burn Disc. Just like magic (it's not really magic), iTunes begins to burn the playlist to your disc. When iTunes finishes copying your music you'll hear a notification sound and your new disc will appear in the Source pane. If at any time you want to stop or cancel the burning process, click the X button on the right of the status display window.

NOTE: You cannot copy music to a CD from the iTunes Library. You can only burn to CD by first selecting a playlist.

The "Almost an iPod in Your Car" Trick

If you don't have a way to connect your iPod to your car's stereo, my buddy Terry White (a certified iPod freak) came up with the next best thing. Here's his plan: You create a giant playlist with all your favorite songs (let's say it's 340 songs, and if you're like Terry, it's mostly Spice Girls, Hanson, and 98 Degrees). Instead of putting the 340 songs on your iPod, click on your playlist, hit the Random button, then press the Burn button. Now, I know what you're thinking: "You're not going to fit 340 songs on a CD." That's right, unless they're very, very short songs, and that's the secret (kidding). iTunes will create a series of CDs, and when the first one is full, it will eject it—you pop in another, and it'll keep creating CD after CD until all 340 songs are burned, and then you can listen to your iTunes playlist in your car without your Mac or an iPod.

Be Selective when Burning

If you don't want to copy certain songs in your playlist when burning a disc, simply uncheck the song in the playlist and iTunes will skip it…not copy it…completely ignore it…avoid it like the plague. In other words, it won't be burned to your CD.

Burning MP3 CDs

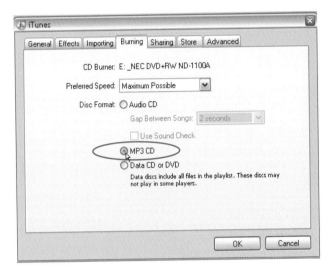

If your CD player will play MP3 music files, then you may want to choose to burn your songs as MP3s. Since MP3 uses compression, you'll be able to burn more songs to a single disc. To do this, press Ctrl-, (comma) to open the preference dialog and click the Burning tab. Next, click MP3 CD, listed under Disc Format, and click OK. Now, all songs burned to disc will be copied as MP3s.

Adjust the Gap

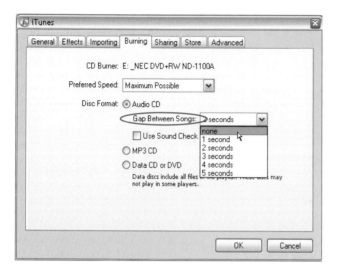

When you burn songs to disc, iTunes automatically sets a two-second gap (pause) between each track. However, you may want to adjust this gap depending on the music or the mood you're trying to create. Press Ctrl-, (comma) to open the preference dialog, click the Burning tab, and under Disc Format click the Gap Between Songs pop-up menu. Choose from None to 5 Seconds. Click OK and your songs will be burned with the selected gap between songs.

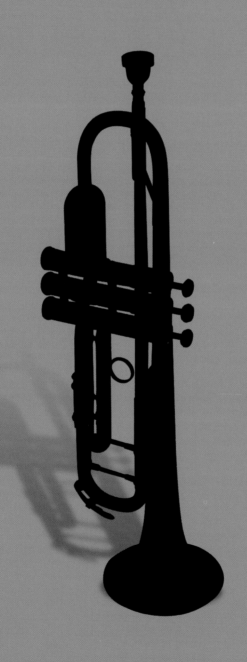

Chapter Seven

Portable People

Using iTunes with Your iPod

Portable People? OK, it's a stretch, but if you think about it, the iPod is about making your iTunes music portable. That's why we searched for a song with the word "portable" in the title, and luckily for us, the band Ten Years After recorded a song with that very title, which we're delighted to use here. Even better, "Portable People" is available in the iTunes Music Store. I just previewed it, and I have to say, I don't really hate it. It would make an ideal title song for a UPN sitcom about life in the late 60s to early 70s. Now, strange as this may sound, there are songs that contain the word "pod" (not iPod mind you, but just "pod"), and we considered using one of those. They included "Back to the Pod" from the soundtrack of John Carpenter's hit movie *Escape from New York*. (A lot of people don't realize that John Carpenter is also a composer, and wrote the score for *Escape from New York* himself, as he did many of his other movies. Why am I telling you this? I have no idea.) We also looked at "Death Pod" by Gwar from their album *Scumdogs of the Universe*. I dunno, although "Death Pod" makes a great name for a song, as a chapter title, it just loses something. We then looked at "Inside My Pod" (which I personally liked) by Busker Soundcheck (sadly, the album is out of print), but when all was said and done, we went with "Portable People." Partially because if you got hung up on the title, you could download the song from the iTunes Music Store and at the very least, preview it and say, "Hey, that would make a great theme song for a UPN sitcom."

Putting Songs on Your iPod

iTunes was made to work seamlessly with the iPod—you realize just how dynamic this duo really is the first time you connect your iPod to your PC. The iPod, by default, automatically syncs with iTunes. So, to copy your music and playlists onto your iPod, simply connect the iPod to your PC. iTunes automatically begins transferring your iTunes Library and playlists onto your iPod. Each time you connect your iPod to your computer, iTunes will update it with any changes that you've made to your iTunes Library and playlists. Naturally (as with all the tips in this chapter), this applies to the iPod mini as well as the original iPod.

How Much Space?

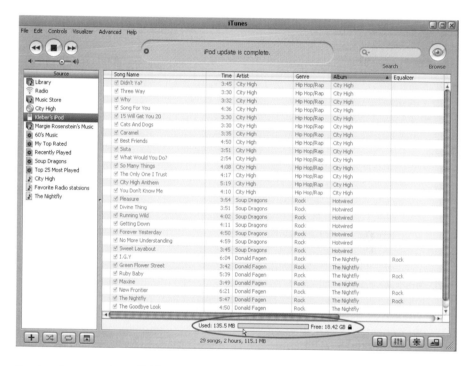

To view how much available space you have on your iPod, select your iPod in the iTunes Source pane, then glance down at the bottom center of the iTunes windows. This display shows exactly how much space has been used and how much free space remains. This is useful for making certain that you have enough space to hold all of your music. If you don't, then you may want to deselect songs that you don't want transferred to your iPod to free up space and ensure that all of the music you do want gets transferred properly.

Manually Update Your iPod

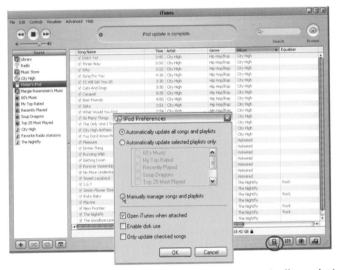

Maybe you don't like the idea of iTunes automatically updating your iPod, and who can blame you—I'm not that crazy about programs thinking for me, either. Actually, it can be a pain allowing iTunes to automatically update your iPod each time you connect to your computer. Well, you can turn off this helpful nuisance. To turn off auto-updating, click the iPod Preferences button located at the bottom right of the iTunes window (this button only appears when your iPod is connected to your computer) and select Manually Manage Songs and Playlists, then click OK. You can also choose to be selective and have iTunes update only selected playlists by selecting Automatically Update Selected Playlists Only and then checking the playlist(s) from the menu. A small triangle now appears to the left of your iPod in iTunes' Source pane. Click this triangle to display the playlists on your iPod. Now, simply drag-and-drop music onto your iPod, iPod mini, or any playlist.

Cool Tip
An easy way to tell whether or not you're using automatic update is to look at the iTunes Song list when your iPod is selected in the Source pane. When automatic update is active, the Song list text appears faded. If you're using manual update, the Song list's text appears normal (not faded), allowing you to drag–and–drop music files to your iPod.

iPortable Hard Drive

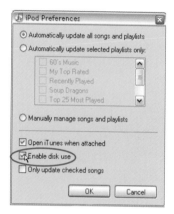

Apple's iPod does a lot more than just carry around your music; it's also a portable hard drive. After all, it does have a 20–40-GB hard drive. To make your iPod a drag-and-drop drive, click the iPod Preferences button and check Enable Disk Use, then click OK. Your iPod now appears in My Computer as a removable storage device. Now, you can drag-and-drop files and applications or back up your entire hard drive and carry it with you wherever you go. Pretty cool, huh?

NOTE: When Enable Disc Use is active, you must manually "unmount" your iPod before each disconnect. Which basically means you must manually eject it before removing the iPod from its base. To eject your iPod, Right-click your iPod's name in the iTunes Source pane and select Eject iPod from the shortcut menu.

iPod–Only Playlists

You may want to create playlists on your iPod or iPod mini that you wouldn't necessarily want in iTunes. For example, you may want a couple of smaller workout playlists to use at the gym. These would be needed on your iPod but not necessarily in iTunes. Well, iTunes allows you to do this. First, make certain that you have selected to manually update your iPod (you cannot add playlists to your iPod when automatic update is active). Select your iPod in iTunes' Source pane, then click the Create a Playlist button, found at the bottom left of the window. This displays the playlist on your iPod and creates a new playlist, ready to be named. Now, simply drag-and-drop music to your new playlist and you're set. You just created an iPod-only playlist.

Accessorize

Do you want to add voice notes to your iPod, add external speakers, or even transmit your iPod's songs through an FM radio? Then go to Apple's website (www.apple.com/ipod/accessories.html) and check out their iPod accessories. They have all types of cool add-ons for your iPod. It really is worth a look and can make your iPod more than just a portable music player.

Beat the Alphabet

If you want certain playlists to appear first in your iPod's playlist menu, you can do this by renaming a playlist with an asterisk (*) in front of its title. For example, if your favorite playlist is "Zippy Tunes" (sorry, couldn't think of anything that started with a "z"), which would automatically appear in alphabetical order at the bottom of your playlist menu, then rename this playlist with an asterisk in front of the title and it will appear in the first position of your iPod's playlist menu. Repeat this to make as many playlists as you like appear at the top of the playlist line-up.

NOTE: This can be done by either renaming the playlist in iTunes and updating your iPod automatically, or by renaming the playlist manually on your iPod.

Give Your iPod a New Name

To rename your iPod or iPod mini, click its name in the iTunes Source pane to select it, and click once more directly on the name's text to edit the name field. Now, give your iPod a new name and then press Enter on your keyboard when finished. iTunes will update your iPod and your new name will appear in the Source pane.

Rating Songs Goes Both Ways

I'm sure you probably already know that if you rate a song using iTunes, that song rating is carried forth into your iPod or iPod mini; however, it also works the other way around. If instead you rate a song in your iPod, when you sync back to iTunes, the ratings you assigned in your iPod are now updated in iTunes. It's a two-way thing, baby!

Your iPod as Voice Recorder

If you bought one of the third-party mics that let you turn your iPod into a fancy-schmancy voice recorder, iTunes is totally hip to that (that's jazz lingo) and when you sync up, iTunes will sync the notes on your iPod with any voice notes you've made on your computer.

Add "Group" Words to Make Portable Song Lists

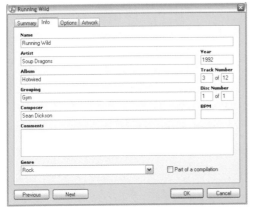

Apple snuck a new little feature in iTunes 4.2 that is kind of like keywords, but the info is embedded into the song's MP3 info, so it moves from computer to computer. Like keywords, it's designed to help make Smart Playlists even easier. It's called "Grouping" and what it's designed to do is let you assign your own smart words to songs (almost like creating your own custom genre). For example, let's say that you're playing a song and think, "This would be great for my workout at the gym." If so, click on the song, then press Control-I to bring up iTunes' Info window and click on the Info tab. That's where you'll find the Grouping field. Enter "Gym" and that song is now tagged as one of the songs you want to hear at the gym. Then, once you have enough songs tagged as Gym, you can quickly make a Smart Playlist of just the songs you want to take to the gym based on their grouping. You can sync this playlist to your iPod or iPod mini and then head to the gym, fully loaded (I don't mean to make it sound like you're drunk when you head to the gym, but if you are, then it really fits).

Finding "Unrated" Songs on Your iPod

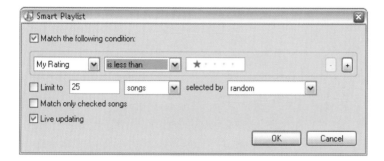

Chances are you have songs on your iPod or iPod mini that don't have ratings. If you're into making Smart Playlists, you probably want to give all your songs a rating, even if they're bad ratings (one star). Luckily, you don't have to search song by song. Instead, create a Smart Playlist in iTunes, then when the Smart Playlist dialog appears, choose these criteria: In the first pop-up menu, choose My Rating; for the second, choose Is Less Than; and then in the last field, click on the first star to choose only one star. Click OK and it creates a playlist with all the songs rated less than one star (in other words, a playlist of all your unrated songs). Now, you can quickly rate these songs, then sync just to your iPod and it will update your unranked iPod songs with your new rankings.

Chapter Eight

Silver Screen Shower Scene

iTunes Visuals

iTunes lets you have an onscreen psychedelic experience that Jimi Hendrix would've been proud of. It's called the "Visualizer" and believe it or not, we found not one, but four songs named exactly that— "Visualizer." One by Andy Seidler, two by Visuddha (one was a dance mix), and one by a band of the same name—Visualizer. So why didn't we go with Visualizer as our chapter name? Well, two reasons: (1) It's too short, and (2) it's too obvious. Now, I think you'd agree that the title "Silver Screen Shower Scene" is neither too short, nor too obvious, and it contains the word "Screen," which is what the iTunes Visualizer takes over when you start it. Now, you're probably thinking (because you previewed the song "Rip Session" earlier, with its naughty lyrics) that any song with the term "Shower Scene" in it is probably naughty, too. I don't think it is (it doesn't contain the "Explicit Lyrics" warning anyway) and I previewed it in the iTunes Music Store and liked it. But there's a third reason we chose it. The song is by a group named Felix da Housecat, and our Creative Director is named Felix (Felix Nelson) and so we took that as a sign and went with it. As luck would have it, "Silver Screen Shower Scene" (the "Ladytron Live at Eric's Mix") is the perfect song to play as you watch the iTunes Visualizer. In fact, there's a reasonable chance that if you buy that song, play it, then run the Visualizer, you'll black out (numerous times, in fact) and when you wake up you will have achieved full and total inner consciousness. Hey, stranger things have happened.

Get Funky

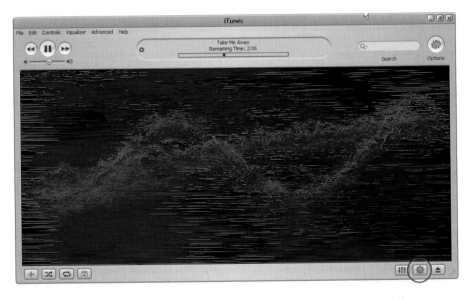

Chances are, you're not a child of the sixties, but I bet your parents are and if you want to see what life was like for them when they were young, press Ctrl-T, or click the Visualizer button on the bottom right of the iTunes window. This turns on iTunes funk. iTunes visual effects are synced to songs currently playing and display an effect you'd expect to see projected behind bands like Cream and Jefferson Airplane during concerts back when people smoked anything that wasn't tied down. I actually like this psychedelic blast-from-the-past; heck, sometimes I turn it on simply as a form of personal punishment. However, as best I can tell, the reason this mind-bending visual display is included in iTunes is that Apple figures many iTunes users will at some point want to (a) start burning some incense and then (b) call Pizza Hut delivery. I can honestly say that although I've done option "b" quite a number of times, I've yet to try option "a."

Maximize Your Funk

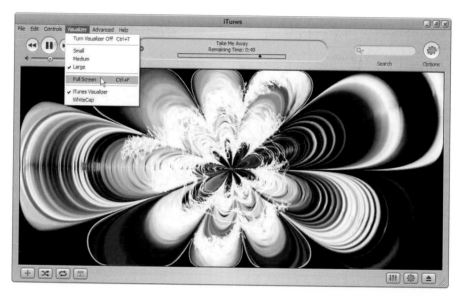

Okay, it's time to get really trippy and maximize the funk. When the visual effects are playing, press Ctrl-F to take 'em full screen, and the effect takes over your entire screen (and perhaps your entire life). Yeah, makes you want to break out the Pink Floyd, doesn't it? Press Ctrl-F again for the visual effects to show only in your iTunes window; or to get back your normal iTunes window, simply press Escape (Esc) on your keyboard.

iLogo (The Hidden Corporate Message)

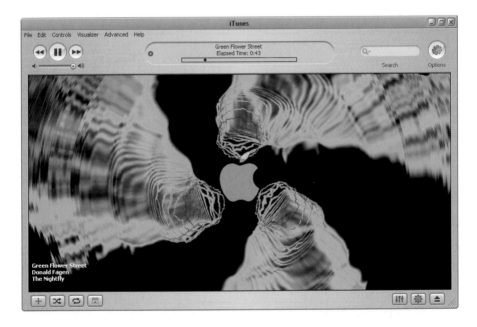

Want to really "mess" with people's heads while they're sucked into the endless vortex of iTunes' psychedelic visuals? Just press the letter "b" while it's turned on and the corporate logo of a giant Fortune 500 company will appear in the center of the visuals and stay there, reminding you that the world is really run by giant corporations and we're powerless to do anything but send them more money and follow their orders. (Okay, pressing "b" really just brings up a white Apple logo center screen, but it sounds much more Orwellian to call it the "corporate logo of a giant Fortune 500 company.")

Visual Effects

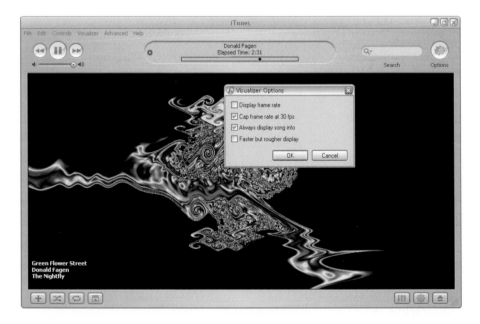

Let's pretend for a moment that iTunes' visual effects are important. And, since we're pretending they're important, we're gonna need a set of options to control their playback, right? Well, sadly, there are options for iTunes visualizations—and when they're active within the iTunes window, their Options button appears in the top right corner of it. These options include adjusting the playback frame rate and displaying the frame rate—you know, critical stuff like that.

Who's Playing?

Want to see the song's info while the visual effects are playing? Click the Options button (while the effects are playing) and check Always Display Song Info, then click OK. Now, the song's name, artist, and album name will always appear in the lower left corner of the window. Even cooler—if you add album art, that's displayed along with the name as well.

One–Key Control

If you're really serious about iTunes' visual effects, you might as well learn how to make this puppy really jump through some hoops. While the visual effects are running, press "?" (the question mark key) on your keyboard to open Basic Visualizer Help—a list of one-key controls for various other features. I know what you're thinking: "If there's 'Basic Help,' then somewhere there must be an 'Advanced Help,' right?" Right!

Gettin' Geeky with Visuals

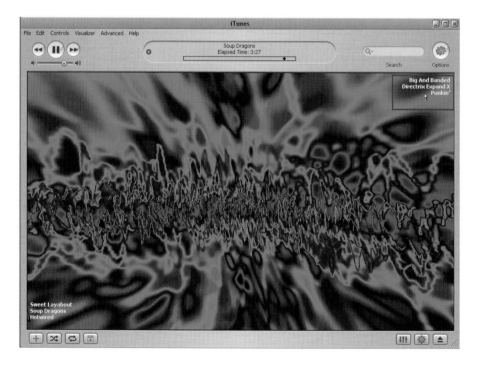

I know how you feel—right about now you're thinking, "The iTunes effects are great, but I need to change it up a little." Good news! You can. Try this: While the visual effects are playing, press "z" on your keyboard. Oh, yeah…we've opened a box of funk now! Continue pressing the "z" key to cycle through, well, a whole bunch (I'm sure that someone somewhere has counted all of them…I'm not going to) of different color combinations, but better yet—iTunes displays the names of these color schemes onscreen. Press the letter "q" to change to wireframe lines that dance to your music. Pressing the letter "a" changes something (I know it's changing, because I see its name changing in the display, but I've yet to figure out what it is; I know that after watching it for just a short time, I get a craving for a bag of Cheetos™).

Plug In to Visual Effects

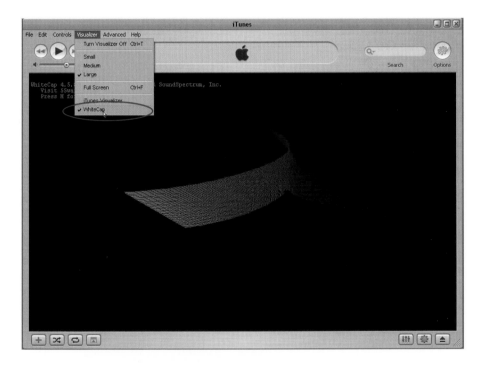

If you're totally sucked into the whole visual effects thing (and I know you are), there are people out there creating their own iTunes visuals and you can download them from the Web (many are free). A good example is a plug-in called WhiteCap (www.55ware.com/whitecap). WhiteCap offers free visualizations for just about every player available, including iTunes. Just download 'em and enjoy, because you really can never have too many visual effects.

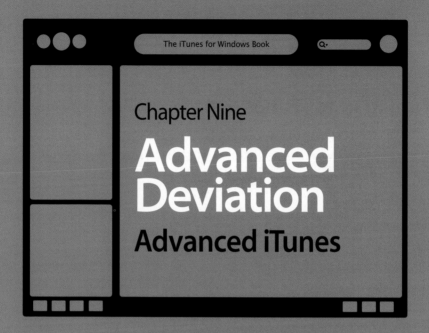

Chapter Nine

Advanced Deviation

Advanced iTunes

OK, you've been through all the basics. You've survived explicit lyrics, blacking out, and the shower scene. Now it's time to learn some really cool iTunes stuff. Now, the title for this chapter, "Advanced Technology," does not seem like it was taken from a song, but in fact, it was. It's a lame name for a song, but it is a song nonetheless, by a band named Empirion, from their album *Advanced Technology* (which isn't a bad name for an album). You can preview it in the iTunes Music Store, but I have to warn you—it's annoying as hell. The preview sounds like just one long repeating synthesizer loop (I have to imagine the full song is better than the 30-second preview, or that song will sit there, undownloaded, until the end of recorded time). But that didn't stop us from using it as the chapter title. Why? Because the other choices were just as bad (the titles, not the songs). There was a song called (I kid you not) "Advanced Malignant Tumor of the Brain." Probably a love song. There was one named "Advanced Manufacturing and Design" by Lesser, and my personal favorite, "Advanced Japanese Candlestick Man" by Doleful Lions. See, Advanced Technology is sounding pretty good right about now, isn't it? Hey, I was just searching and came across a pretty good song title called "Advanced Deviation" by Haujobb. That actually would have been a better name for this chapter. In fact, I think I'm going to go change the chapter name to Advanced Deviation right now, so forget all the "Advanced Technology" stuff I said earlier.

Tuning In to iTunes

iTunes is the perfect tool for playing digital music, but it gets even better when you start playing your favorite radio stations. I'm almost always listening to music while working on my computers, and I've learned that no matter how extensive your iTunes Library of music may be, it's gonna get stale after a while. It just is. Trust me on this, there's just something about listening to the same songs continuously that makes me feel stupid. I find myself staring blankly at the ceiling wondering how many licks it really does take to get to the center of a lollipop. You see, you start losing brain cells left and right. Well, you can prevent this from happening to you (it's too late for me), because you're just a few clicks away from piping in brand-new music from 21 different default genres. Using iTunes, you can tune in to literally thousands of streaming Internet radio stations. Here's how: Click the Radio link in the Source pane to open the Internet Radio genre window. To view a genre's available radio stations, double-click the genre's name or click the triangle to its left. To begin playing a station, simply double-click the station's name.

Hey, Who Did That Song?

How many times have you been listening to the radio and you hear a song that you love, but of course, the DJ never gives the song title or artist's name, so you have no way of getting your hands on the song because you have no idea who it is? I bet this has happened to you a lot; I know it's happened to me way too many times to count. Well, you're in luck. For many (not all) Internet radio stations, iTunes will display song info in the top center of the iTunes window. The song info display shows how long you've been listening to the radio stream, as well as the title and artist name of the song that is currently playing. Now you'll know who and what you're listening to. Yeah, I'm heading to the iTunes Music Store (my wife will be thrilled).

My Favorite Radio Stations

Now that you've found the joy of streaming Internet radio stations, you're going to want to keep track of your favorites. You can do this by creating a playlist. Click the Create A Playlist button at the bottom left of the iTunes window, then give your new playlist a name (something like "Favorite Radio Stations"). Now, simply drag-and-drop your favorite radio stations into it, just like you would drag-and-drop music files into playlists. So now, any time you want to quickly get to your favorite radio stations, they're just a click away.

NOTE: Since an Internet radio station streams (plays) continuously, iTunes will not advance to the next station as it does with music files in other playlists. Double-click a radio station in your playlist to switch radio stations.

It's Good to Share

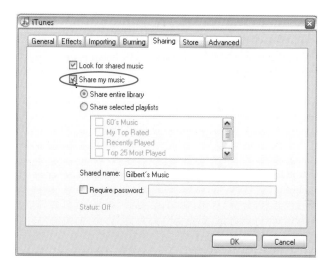

iTunes makes it easy to share and play music on your home or office network. For example, at my home we have several computers on the network and everyone's able to play music from the server. This makes giving everyone access to the songs in my iTunes Library quick and easy. This also prevents me from having to place copies of my songs on each computer and then having to continuously update the folder when I add new music. And, best of all, you can choose which of your play-lists users can access from your iTunes Library. Here's how: Press Ctrl-, (comma) to open the preference dialog and select the Sharing tab. Next, check Share My Music and select to either share your entire Library or to share individual playlists, then click OK. You can also require a password to access your music Library just in case you don't want to share with everyone on your network.

Keep It Simple—Import Your Playlists

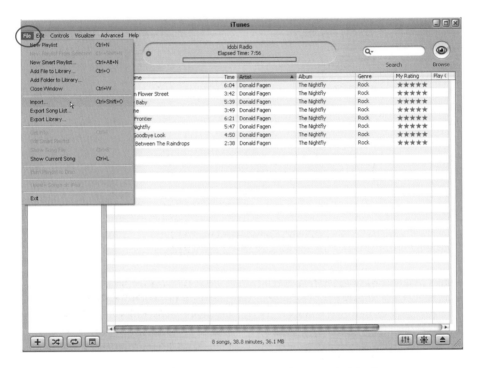

Chances are you have more than one computer and you probably share your songs between 'em. Well, there's no need to create the same playlists for each computer. Simply import your playlists to each computer instead. First, export your playlists—as explained earlier—by Right-clicking the Library or a playlist in the Source pane and selecting Export Song List in the shortcut menu. Choose a location on your hard drive to save the playlist (e.g., Desktop) and click Save. Now, to import your playlists, copy them to your other computer(s), then choose File>Import in the iTunes menu. Using the Import dialog, locate the playlists on your hard drive and click Open, which places the playlist in the iTunes Source pane, ready to be used.

NOTE: Importing playlists only copies the playlist's song info from computer to computer, and not the actual song files. To play the music listed in the playlist, make certain that you have copies of the songs on each computer.

Another Way to Shuffle

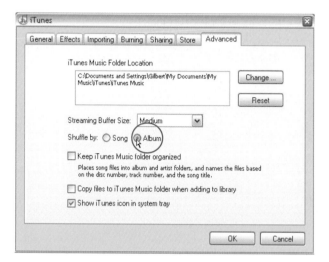

By now, you know how to shuffle songs in your Library or in a playlist. But there's another way to shuffle your music in iTunes—you can also shuffle by Album. Try this: Press Ctrl-, (comma) to open the preference menu and click the Advanced tab. Next, select Album (to the right of Shuffle By), then click OK. Now, when you select shuffle, iTunes will play an entire album in its original song order and then randomly select the next album to play.

Convert Your Songs

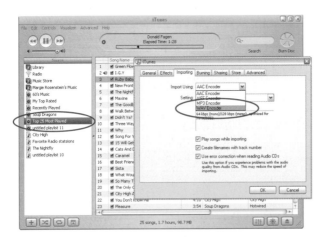

Here's a very cool, little-known iTunes tip for converting a song's format. Let's say you import all of your music using iTunes MP3 Encoder format, but now you want to convert those songs to a WAV format to create a disc that you can play in any CD player. You can do this in iTunes by first pressing Ctrl-, (comma) to open the preference dialog and clicking the Importing tab. Next, select the encoding format that you want to convert the song to (e.g., WAV Encoder) from the Import Using pop-up menu, then click OK. Now, select the song or songs in your Library that you want to convert. Right-click the selected song(s) and click Convert Selection to WAV in the shortcut menu. Your song(s) will now begin the conversion and inform you when complete. Each converted song will appear directly below the originally selected song(s).

NOTE: You cannot convert music purchased from the iTunes Music Store. Songs purchased through the iTunes Music Store are encoded using a protected AAC format that will not allow them to be converted.

Cool Tip

To save the converted songs to a different location on your hard drive (other than the iTunes music folder) hold the Shift key when clicking Convert Selection to WAV in the shortcut menu. This opens the Browse for Folder dialog, allowing you to quickly save the music files anywhere on your hard drive.

Index

A

AAC encoding, 91
AAC format, 91, 134
accessories, iPod, 109
Account button, 81–82
Add Song button, 65, 74
Advanced icon, 85
Advanced tab, 133
AIFF encoding, 91
AIFF format, 91–92
Album option, 133
albums
    artwork for, 27, 122
    finding, 50, 76
    playing, 133
    renaming, 9
    shuffling, 133
    sorting music by, 51
    titles, 2–4, 9, 50
AllMusic.com website, 27
"Allowance" feature, 70
Always Display Song Info option, 122
Apple logo, 120
Apple website, 109
Artist column, 72, 79–80
artists
    browsing, 79
    discography, 77
    finding songs by, 50, 72, 76
    finding websites for, 77
    Internet radio and, 129
    name of, 3–4, 9, 129
    renaming, 9
    song versions and, 71
    sorting music by, 51
artwork, album, 27, 122
Artwork box, 27
asterisk (*), 110
audio
    balance, 21
    compression, 91–92
    formats. See formats
    frequency, 22
    muting, 20
    quality of, 22, 91–92
    streaming, 67
    volume, 20–21
audio CDs. See CDs
audio files
    compression, 91
    copying to iTunes Music Folder, 53
    dragging to playlists, 95
    finding on hard disk, 60
    MP3, 88, 91–92, 114
    size of, 5, 91–92
audio frequency, 22
audio streams, 67
Authorize Computer command, 68
automatic imports, 94
automatic updates, 39, 104, 106
Automatically Update Selected Playlists Only
        option, 106

B

Back button, 78
balance, 21
bass sliders, 22
Billboard's Hot 100 songs, 83
Browse button, 51, 79
browsers, 69, 77
browsing
    artists, 79
    genres, 52, 79
    iTunes Music Store, 79
    Library, 51–52
    songs, 51–52, 79
buffer, 85
Burn Disc button, 97
burning CDs, 97–101
    canceling burns, 97
    eliminating gaps between tracks, 101
    file size and, 5
    formatting options, 100–101
    MP3 CDs, 100
    one-button burning, 97
    playlists, 29, 97–99
    selecting/deselecting songs, 29
    series of CDs from iPod, 98
    skipping songs, 99
Burning tab, 100–101
Buy and Download Using
        1-Click option, 74
Buy Now button, 65, 74
Buy Song button, 65, 74

C

CDDB Internet audio database, 90
CDNOW.com website, 27
CDs
    burning. See burning CDs

CDs (continued)
covers for, 47
damaged, 96
ejecting, 94
insertion of, 2, 94, 97
MP3, 100
name of, 2, 90
renaming, 9
Clear command, 10, 35–36
color schemes, visual effects, 124
columns
adding, 8
Artist, 72, 79–80
dragging, 13
Equalizer, 24
fitting in windows, 16
Genre, 79
My Rating, 42–43, 59, 115
Play Count, 45
rearranging, 13
Relevance, 80
removing, 8
restoring, 16
reversing order of, 14
Song list, 7–8, 13
Song Name, 13
sorting, 14
turning on/off, 7–8
views, 7–8, 13
commands
Authorize Computer, 68
Clear, 10, 35–36
Consolidate Library, 54
Deauthorize Computer, 68
Eject iPod, 107
Export Song List, 47, 132
Get CD Track Names, 90
Get Info, 4, 58, 88–89
Import, 132
Import Songs and Eject, 94
Join CD Tracks, 93
New Playlist, 34
New Playlist From Selection, 41
Reset Play Count, 45
Show Artwork, 27
Show Song File, 60
Show Songs, 94
composers
finding songs by, 76
name of, 4
compression
MP3 files, 91–92
sound quality and, 91–92

computers
authorizing, 68, 84
copying song info between, 132
deauthorizing, 68
importing playlists, 132
preventing others from buying songs, 81
sharing music between, 131
syncing with iPod, 104, 113, 115
volume, 20–21
Connect To Internet When Needed
option, 90
connections
as-needed, 90
dial-up, 67
high-speed Internet, 85
Consolidate Library command, 54
Copy Files to iTunes Music Folder option, 53
copying items
audio files to iTunes Music Folder, 53
HTML code, 69
song info between computers, 132
songs on hard disk, 53–54
songs/playlists to iPod, 104
covers, CD, 47
Create Playlist button, 34, 40, 108, 130
Crossfade Playback option, 30
crossfading, 30
Ctrl key, 11
customization. *See also* **presets**
EQs, 23–25
font size, 56
genres, 55
Top 10 playlist, 39

D

Deauthorize Computer command, 68
Delete key, 10–11, 35
deleting items
canceling deletion, 10
columns, 8
playlists, 36
songs from Library, 10–11
songs from playlists, 35
dial-up connections, 67
digital EQ meter, 6
Disc Format options, 100–101
discography, 77
discs. *See also* **CDs**
damaged, 96
ejecting, 94
insertion of, 2, 94, 97
disks. *See* **hard disk**
downloaded songs, 31, 67–68
downloads, one-click, 65, 74

E

editing
   MP3 tags, 88
   multiple songs, 58
   song info, 4, 9, 58, 88
   song intros, 57
   song tags, 89
effects, visual, 117–125
Effects tab, 21, 30
Eject iPod command, 107
ejecting CDs, 94
ejecting iPod, 107
Elapsed Time display, 3
Enable Disk Use option, 107
encoding items, 91, 134
EQ meter, 6, 23
equalizer, graphic, 22–25
Equalizer column, 24
Equalizer Preset menu, 25
error correction, 96
Escape key, 119
Explicit warnings, 73
Export Song List command, 47, 132
exporting items
   playlist info as text, 47
   songs, 47, 132
external speakers, 109

F

files
   compression, 91
   copying to iTunes Music Folder, 53–54
   dragging to playlists, 95
   finding on hard disk, 60
   MP3, 88, 91–92, 114
   size of, 6, 91–92
   tab-delimited text, 47
finding
   albums, 50, 76
   artist websites, 77
   artists, 50, 72, 76
   audio files on hard disk, 60
   CD track names, 90
   CDDB information, 90
   composers, 76
   genres, 50, 76, 79
   hidden Music Store links, 72
   Music Store Power Search, 76
   by Relevance, 80
   song versions, 71
   songs, 50, 60, 72, 76
   unrated songs on iPod, 115
five-star playlists, 43

FM radio, 109
folders
   iTunes Music, 53
   iTunes Wish List, 64
font size, song list, 56
formats
   AAC, 91, 134
   AIFF, 91–92
   Disc Format options, 100
   MP3, 91–92, 134
   unable to convert, 134
   WAV, 92
frame rates, 121
frequency, 22

G

Gap Between Songs settings, 101
General tab, 52, 56
Genre column, 79
genres
   browsing by, 52, 79
   custom, 55
   EQ settings, 24
   finding, 50, 76, 79
   multiple, 55
   preset, 55
   radio stations, 128
   searching by, 79
Get CD Track Names command, 90
Get Info command, 4, 58, 88–89
graphic equalizer (EQ), 22–25
grouping songs, 114

H

hard disk
   consolidating songs on, 54
   copying songs on, 53–54
   iPod as, 107
   locating songs on, 60
   saving music files to, 134
hiding iTunes, 20
high-speed Internet connections, 85
Hot 100 songs, 83
HTML code, 69

I

Import command, 132
Import Songs and Eject command, 94
Import Using menu, 91–92
importing items. *See also* **ripping songs**
   auto-importing music, 94
   damaged CDs, 96

importing items *(continued)*
eliminating gaps, 93
gaps between tracks and, 93
joining tracks and, 93
options for, 92
playlists, 132
quality of, 91, 96
slower method of, 96
songs to playlists, 95
Importing tab, 92, 96
Info tab, 4, 88–89
Internet
CDDB service, 90
connections, 67, 85, 90
streaming from, 85
Internet radio, 128–130
Internet Radio genre window, 128
intros, song, 57
iPod, 103–115
accessories, 109
burning series of CDs from, 98
connecting to car stereo, 98
copying songs/playlists to, 104
creating playlists on, 108
displaying playlists on, 106
ejecting, 107
external speakers for, 109
FM radio add-on, 109
as hard disk, 107
microphones for, 113
MP3 format and, 92
playlist order, 110
removing from base, 107
renaming, 111
song ratings and, 112, 115
space available on, 105
syncing with computer, 104, 113, 115
syncing with iTunes, 104, 115
unmounting, 107
unranked songs on, 115
updating automatically, 104, 106
updating manually, 106
as voice recorder, 109, 113
iPod-only playlists, 108
iPod Preferences button, 106
iTunes
advanced features, 127–134
basics, 1–17
column display in, 7–8, 13
controlling from Taskbar, 26
deleting songs from, 10–11
hiding, 20
muting, 20
radio stations, 128–130

resizing windows in, 16
restoring player size, 17
shortcut menu, 26
shrinking player, 17
syncing iPod with, 104, 115
volume controls, 20–21
iTunes icon, 26
iTunes Link Maker, 69
iTunes Music folder, 53–54
iTunes Music Store, 63–85
Account button, 81–82
Add Song button, 65, 74
adding songs to Library, 31
allowance for, 70
authorizing computer, 68, 84
Billboard's Hot 100 songs, 83
browsing, 79
Buy Now button, 65, 74
Buy Song button, 65, 74
deauthorizing computer, 68
finding artist websites, 77
hidden links in, 73
home page navigation, 75
linking webpages to songs, 69
live links in, 73
one-click downloads, 65, 74
Power Search, 76
preventing others from buying songs, 81
previewing song charges, 65
purchase history, 82
sharing music and, 84
Shopping Cart feature, 65, 74
shortcuts, 78
signing out of, 81
song previews, 67, 71, 85
sorting searches, 80
telling friends about songs, 66
unable to convert music, 134
"wish list," 64
iTunes Visualizer, 117–125

J

Join CD Tracks command, 93
joining/unjoining tracks, 93

K

keyboard shortcuts. *See also* **shortcuts**
full-screen visual effects, 119
jumping to playing songs, 15
Show Artwork command, 27
Smart Playlist creation, 40
View Options dialog, 7
visual effects, 123

L

Library
adding songs to, 31
browsing, 51–52
consolidating songs in, 54
deleting songs from, 10–11
password for, 131
repeating playlists/songs in, 28
running time, 5
selecting songs in, 2
sharing, 131
song order in, 12
links
artist websites, 77
Explicit warnings, 73
hidden Music Store links, 72
iTunes Link Maker, 69
linking webpages to songs, 69
live Music Store links, 73
Radio link, 128
Tell a Friend link, 73
Load Complete Preview Before Playing
option, 67
logo, Apple, 120

M

Manually Manage Songs and Playlists
option, 106
Maximize/Restore button, 16–17
meter, EQ, 6, 23
microphone, 113
midrange sliders, 22
Mini-tunes player, 17
Most Often Played option, 39
MP3 CDs, 100
MP3 files
compression and, 91–92
grouping and, 114
tagging, 88
MP3 format, 91–92, 134
MP3 tags, 88
Multiple Song Information dialog, 25, 58
music. See also songs
available space on iPod, 105
browsing, 51–52
Explicit warnings, 73
formats. See formats
genre, 52, 55
importing. See importing
muting, 20
organizing, 49–60
playing. See playing music
previewing, 67, 71, 85

purchasing. See iTunes Music Store
sharing, 84, 131
shuffling, 12, 133
Tell a Friend option, 66
unable to convert format, 134
visual effects, 117–125
music CDs. See CDs
music library. See Library
Music Store. See iTunes Music Store
muting iTunes, 20
My Rating column, 42–43, 59, 115

N

networks
playing songs over, 131
sharing music over, 84, 131
New Playlist command, 34
New Playlist From Selection command, 41
Next button, 89
notes, syncing, 113

O

On CD Insert settings, 94
one-click downloads, 65, 74
Options button, 121–122
Options tab, 57
organizing music, 49–60

P

passwords, Library, 131
pausing songs, 2
play button, 2
play count, songs, 39, 45
Play Count column, 45
Play Count settings, 39
Play Songs After Downloading option, 67
playback frame rate, 121
players
Mini-tunes, 17
restoring size, 17
visual effects plug-ins, 125
playing music
albums, 133
crossfading, 30
over networks, 131
radio stations, 128
from server, 131
shuffling albums, 133
shuffling songs, 12
song previews, 67
songs, 2, 67, 131
tracks, 2

playlists, 33–47
  adding songs to, 34
  automatic updates, 39, 104, 106
  burning to CD, 97–99
  combining, 46
  copying to iPod, 104
  creating, 34, 40–41, 108, 130
  crossfading between songs, 30
  deleting, 36
  deleting songs from, 35
  deselecting songs in, 29
  displaying on iPod, 106
  dragging songs/files to, 95
  exporting as text, 47
  five-star, 43
  importing, 132
  importing songs to, 95
  on iPod, 108
  length of, 5
  naming, 34, 110
  opening in new window, 44
  order of, 110
  play time, 5
  radio stations, 130
  rearranging song order, 12
  Recently Played, 38
  renaming, 110
  repeating, 28
  reversing order, 14
  running time, 5
  selecting songs in, 2, 29
  sharing, 131
  showing current song, 15
  size of, 5, 37
  skipping songs in, 37, 99
  smart. See Smart Playlists
  song count, 5
  statistics, 5
  Top 10 custom playlist, 39
  Top 25 Most Played, 38
  updating on iPod, 104, 106
plug-ins, 125
Power Search feature, 76
presets. See also customization
  EQ, 22–23, 25
  genres, 55
previews
  garbled, 67
  iTunes Music Store, 67, 71, 85
  previewing songs, 67, 71, 85
  shortcut for, 71
Previous button, 89
Purchase History button, 82

R

radio, iPod as, 109
Radio link, 128
radio stations, 128–130
random play, 12
rating songs, 42–43, 59, 112, 115
Recently Played playlist, 38
recorder, voice, 113
Relevance column, 80
Remaining Time display, 3
Repeat Playlist/Song button, 28
Reset Play Count command, 45
ripping songs, 87. See also importing items

S

search window, 50
searches
  albums, 50, 76
  artist websites, 77
  artists, 50, 72, 76
  audio files on hard disk, 60
  CD track names, 90
  CDDB information, 90
  composers, 76
  genres, 50, 76, 79
  hidden Music Store links, 72
  Music Store Power Search, 76
  by Relevance, 80
  song versions, 71
  songs, 50, 60, 72, 76
  sorting searches, 77
  unrated songs on iPod, 115
server, playing music from, 131
Set Up an iTunes Allowance page, 70
Share My Music option, 131
sharing music, 84, 131
sharing over network, 131
Sharing tab, 131
Shift key, 11, 40
Shopping Cart feature, 65, 74
shortcut menu, 26, 35
shortcuts. See also keyboard shortcuts
  finding artist's work, 72
  ITMS home page navigation, 75
  iTunes Music Store, 78
  music preview, 71
  vs. Back button, 78
Show Artwork command, 27
Show Genre When Browsing option, 52
Show Song File command, 60
Show Songs command, 94
Shuffle button, 12
Shuffle By option, 133

shuffling music, 12, 133
Sign Out button, 81
Smart Playlist dialog, 39, 43, 115
Smart Playlists
    creating, 39–40
    default, 46
    described, 38
    grouping, 114
    Most Often Played, 39
    ratings and, 115
    Recently Played, 38
    shortcut for, 40
    Top 10, 39
    Top 25, 38
song formats
    AAC, 91, 134
    AIFF, 91–92
    Disc Format options, 100
    MP3, 91–92, 134
    unable to convert, 134
    WAV, 92
song info
    adding, 4
    copying between computers, 132
    displaying, 7
    editing, 4, 9, 58, 88
    Internet radio stations, 129
    MP3 tags, 88
    visual effects and, 122
Song Information dialog, 55
Song list
    column display in, 7–8, 13
    increasing font size, 56
    renaming fields in, 9
song lists, portable, 114
Song Name column, 13
Song Text settings, 56
songs. *See also* **music; tracks**
    adding to Library, 31
    adding to playlists, 34
    album artwork for, 27
    artists. *See* **artists**
    assigning smart words to, 114
    authorizing computer for, 68, 84
    automatic updates, 39, 104, 106
    Billboard's Hot 100, 83
    browsing, 51–52, 79
    buying online. *See* **iTunes Music Store**
    CDDB service, 90
    converting format of, 134
    copying to iPod, 104
    copying to iTunes Music folder, 53–54
    creating playlists from selections, 41
    crossfading between, 30
    custom EQs for, 24–25
    deauthorizing computer for, 68
    deleting from Library, 10–11
    deleting from playlists, 35
    deselecting in playlists, 29
    downloaded, 31, 67–68
    downloaded from other music
        providers, 31
    dragging to playlists, 95
    editing long intros, 57
    editing multiple, 58
    editing tags, 88
    elapsed time, 3
    EQ meter, 6
    EQs for, 24–25
    Explicit warnings, 73
    finding, 50, 60, 72, 76
    five-star, 43
    formats. *See* **formats**
    gaps between, 93, 101
    genre, 52, 55
    grouping, 114
    on hard disk, 53–54, 60
    importing. *See* **importing**
    jumping to playing song, 15
    jumping to previous/next, 89
    length of, 3
    linking webpages to, 69
    most often played, 39
    muting, 20
    name of, 3–4, 9, 50, 90, 129
    organizing, 49–60
    pausing, 2
    play count, 39, 45
    playing. *See* **playing music**
    previews, 67, 71, 85
    rating, 42–43, 59, 112, 115
    rearranging play order, 12
    remaining time, 3
    renaming, 9
    repeating, 28
    resetting play count, 45
    ripping, 87
    selecting in Library, 2
    selecting in playlists, 2, 29
    setting up allowance for purchasing, 70
    sharing, 84, 131
    showing current, 15
    shuffling, 12, 133
    size of, 91–92
    skipping, 37, 99
    tag information, 88–90
    Tell a Friend option, 66
    Top 10, 39

songs *(continued)*
    Top 25, 38
    total time played, 3
    unable to convert format, 134
    unable to find, 50
    updating on iPod, 104, 106
    versions of, 71
    visual effects, 117–125
    volume control, 20–21
    working with, 19–31
sorting music, 51
sorting searches, 80
sound. *See* audio
Sound Check option, 21
Source pane, 97, 132
Spacebar, 2
speakers, 22, 109
Start Time checkbox, 57
stat line, 5
status display, 3, 17
Stop Time checkbox, 57
Store tab, 65, 67
streaming audio, 67
streaming buffer, 85
Streaming Buffer Size settings, 85
streaming Internet radio, 128–130
synchronization, 104, 113, 115

T

tab-delimited text files, 47
tagging MP3 files, 88
tags, song, 88–90
Taskbar, 26
Tell a Friend option, 66
text
    exporting playlists as, 47
    live links, 73
    Song Text settings, 56
time display, 57
Top 10 playlists, 39
Top 25 Most Played playlist, 38
Total Time display, 3
track number, 12–13
tracks. *See also* songs
    gaps between, 93, 101
    joining/unjoining, 93
    name of, 90
    playing. *See* playing music
    viewing, 2

troubleshooting
    damaged CDs, 96
    error correction, 96
    garbled music previews, 67
    unable to convert song format, 134
    unable to find songs, 50

U

Unjoin CD tracks, 93
unmounting iPod, 107
URLs, 64, 66
Use Error Correction When Reading Audio
    CDs option, 96

V

variable bit rate (VBR), 20
View Account button, 82
View Options dialog, 7, 24
visual effects, 117–125
Visual Effects plug-ins, 125
Visualizer, 117–125
Visualizer button, 118
voice notes, 109, 113
voice recorder, 109, 113
volume control, 20–21

W

WAV encoding, 91, 134
WAV format, 92, 134
Web browsers, 69, 77
websites
    album artwork, 27
    AllMusic.com, 27
    Apple, 109
    CDNOW.com, 27
    finding for artists, 77
    HTML code, 69
    linking to songs, 69
    "Tell a Friend" URLs, 66
    visual effects, 125
    WhiteCap, 125
    "wish list" URLs, 64
WhiteCap plug-in, 125
windows
    fitting columns in, 16
    maximizing, 16
    opening playlist in new window, 44
    resizing, 16
    restoring, 16
"wish list" feature, 64

iTunes & the iPod mini! for Mac & Windows!

The best digital jukebox in the world rocks equally well on both Mac and Windows. iTunes for Windows offers a virtual mirror image of the program Mac customers have made one of Apple's greatest hits.

Whether it's importing music from CDs, organizing music into playlists, automatically syncing your music collection between iTunes and your iPod, burning music CDs of your own creation, encoding music in either MP3 or the higher-quality AAC format, listening to audio books and other spoken material, downloading music from the music store, or sharing music between your Mac and PC, iTunes offers the best integrated music experience.

Redefining Your Music Experience!

GRIFFIN & iPod

In perfect harmony

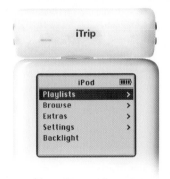

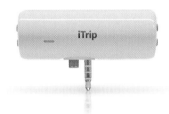

iTrip $35
FM Transmitter for all iPods

- Uses any FM frequency from 87.7 to 107.9
- Powered from iPod - no batteries necessary
- Controlled directly from the iPod
- Available for all iPod models

iTalk $39⁹⁹
Voice Recorder for iPods

- Turns your iPod into a portable voice and memo recorder
- Pass-through jack on top for headphones or separate external microphone
- Built-in microphone and high quality speaker for playback

PowerPod $24⁹⁹
Auto Charger for all iPods

- Works with <u>both</u> New and Original iPods
- Now includes removable Dock-to-FireWire cable
- Charges iPod while playing your music

iPod Cables $14⁹⁹
iPod Home Connection Kit

- Connect your iPod or your Dock to your home stereo or powered speakers
- Kit includes a 6 foot mini-to-RCA cable plus a 7 inch mini-to-RCA female Y-cable

To learn more or order online, visit us at **www.griffintechnology.com**